THE GOSPEL ACCORDING TO PETER

AND

THE REVELATION OF PETER.

𝕷𝖔𝖓𝖉𝖔𝖓: C. J. CLAY AND SONS,
CAMBRIDGE UNIVERSITY PRESS WAREHOUSE,
AVE MARIA LANE.

𝕮𝖆𝖒𝖇𝖗𝖎𝖉𝖌𝖊: DEIGHTON, BELL AND CO.
𝕷𝖊𝖎𝖕𝖟𝖎𝖌: F. A. BROCKHAUS.
𝕹𝖊𝖜 𝖄𝖔𝖗𝖐: MACMILLAN AND CO.

THE GOSPEL
ACCORDING TO PETER, AND
THE REVELATION OF PETER

TWO LECTURES

ON THE NEWLY RECOVERED FRAGMENTS
TOGETHER WITH THE GREEK TEXTS

BY

J. ARMITAGE ROBINSON B.D.

FELLOW AND ASSISTANT TUTOR OF CHRIST'S COLLEGE

AND

MONTAGUE RHODES JAMES M.A.

FELLOW AND DEAN OF KING'S COLLEGE

LONDON: C. J. CLAY AND SONS,
CAMBRIDGE UNIVERSITY PRESS WAREHOUSE,
AVE MARIA LANE.
1892

𝕮𝖆𝖒𝖇𝖗𝖎𝖉𝖌𝖊:

PRINTED BY C. J. CLAY, M.A. AND SONS,
AT THE UNIVERSITY PRESS.

TO

FENTON JOHN ANTHONY HORT D.D.

THE LADY MARGARET'S READER IN DIVINITY

PREFACE.

THE Lecture on the 'Gospel according to Peter' was given in the Hall of Christ's College on the 20th of November, three days after the text was first seen in Cambridge, in response to a general desire for information as to the new discovery. It has since been corrected and enlarged by the addition of some notes, which are placed at the foot of the page, with a view to guiding students to various sources of information which may yet throw further light upon the interpretation of the fragment.

The Lecture on the 'Revelation of Peter' was given before the Divinity Faculty shortly afterwards, and was at the time already in the press.

These editions must be regarded as tentative. Our object has been to place the texts without delay in the hands of other students. We hope that here-after they may be expanded in the series of *Texts and Studies.*

We have to express our best thanks to M. Bouriant, not only for the scholarly way in which he has published the transcription of the MS., but also for the generosity with which he has placed the documents at the disposal of scholars: see p. 147 of

vol. ix. fasc. I. of the Memoirs of the French Archæological Mission at Cairo.

For the rapidity with which this book has been
published, without (we would fain believe) any con-
sequent loss of accuracy in the printing, our thanks
are due to the officers and workmen of the University
Press.

POSTSCRIPT. This little book was finally corrected
for the press when we heard that he, whose latest
message to us was permission to dedicate it to him,
had gone to his rest. It was not without expressions
of misgiving that we had asked to prefix to this hur-
ried work a name which must always be connected
with the minutest accuracy and the most cautious
utterances. It is quite unworthy to be dedicated to
his memory. But we feel that we cannot draw back
or alter now. As here, so there, his gentle spirit will
'make allowance for us'. To his voice we had looked
forward as the one voice which should tell us, as no
other could, where we were right or wrong. Now we
must learn it in a harder school. But it will remain
a sacred duty to carry out these investigations with
the patience and deliberateness which his example
enjoins and his removal has made more than ever
necessary.

J. A. R.
M. R. J.

CAMBRIDGE,
Dec. 1, 1892.

CONTENTS.

THE GOSPEL ACCORDING TO PETER

A LECTURE

ON THE NEWLY RECOVERED FRAGMENT

BY

J. ARMITAGE ROBINSON B.D.

Ἕτερον εὐαγγέλιον, ὃ οὐκ ἔστιν ἄλλο.

THE GOSPEL ACCORDING TO PETER.

WE live in an age of surprises—of surprising recoveries, no less than of surprising inventions. Not to go further back than the last ten years, our knowledge of the early literature of Christianity has been enriched beyond all expectation. In 1883 the Greek Bishop Bryennius gave us the 'Teaching of the Apostles;' and in 1891 Mr Rendel Harris gave us the 'Apology of Aristides.' We knew the fame of both of them with our ears, and when at last we saw them we found that all the time they had both been lurking among us in disguise.

During the past week fragments of three early documents have come to the light: fragments of the Book of Enoch, of the Gospel of Peter and of the Apocalypse of Peter. The Book of Enoch is præ-Christian; it is quoted by S. Jude: we knew it in an Ethiopic Version[1], but we doubted whether we could trust the Version: now we have the first 30 chapters in the Greek itself. The Apocalypse of Peter may go back almost to the end of the first century of our era: Mr M. R. James, of King's, had told some of us what it would contain, if it were ever found:

---

[1] There is also an Old-Sclavonic Version of the Book of Enoch: and a critical edition based on the Versions is now in preparation at Oxford.

now we have a large fragment of it, and we know that he was right.

But perhaps the most startling of our recoveries is that of the 'Gospel according to Peter[1].' What was known of this? Eusebius, 'the Father of Church History,'—who seems so well to have divined what would be of interest to readers who lived fifteen centuries later than his time—mentioned its name, and gave us too a letter of Serapion on its use in church. This letter we must read. It runs as follows (Eus. *H. E.* vi. 12):

'We, brethren, receive Peter and the other Apostles even as Christ; but the writings that go falsely by their names we in our experience reject, knowing that such things as these we never received. When I was with you I supposed you all to be attached to the right faith; and so without going through the Gospel put forward under Peter's name I said: If this is all that makes your petty quarrel[2], why then let it be read. But now that I have learned from information given me that their mind was lurking in some hole of heresy, I will make a point of coming to you again: so, brethren, expect me speedily. Knowing then, brethren, of what kind of heresy was Marcion '—then follows a sentence where the text is faulty: I read 'Marcion' with the Armenian Version[3], against

---

[1] I take the title from Origen, *Comm. in Matth.* x. 17, 'As to the brethren of Jesus, some say on the authority of the Gospel according to Peter (as it is entitled) or of the Book of James, that they were sons of Joseph by a former wife.' Cf. Eus. *H. E.* iii. 3, 2 and 25, 6.

[2] παρέχειν μικροψυχίαν, perhaps 'causes you ill-feeling.'

[3] The Armenian Version, made from a Syriac Version which at this point is no longer extant, runs literally as follows, 'Now, brethren, that (or, 'for') ye see and understand of what heresy was Marcion, that (or 'for') he contradicted himself and that which he spake he

'Marcianus,' an unknown person, of the Greek text 'From others,' he goes on, 'who used this very Gospel,— I mean from the successors of those who started it, whom we call *Docetae ;* for most of its ideas are of their school— from them, I say, I borrowed it and was able to go through it and to find that most of it belonged to the right teaching of the Saviour, but some things were additions.' Thus much, says Eusebius, for Serapion.

Serapion was Bishop of Antioch 190—203, and his letter was addressed to the Church of Rhossos, on the coast just below Antioch. Now if our Gospel be the one referred to by Serapion—and we shall see that it bears out his description—we take it back at once to the 2nd century; and we must allow some years at least for it to gain authority, so that it should be read in church at Rhossos.

Hippolytus, who wrote a Refutation of All Heresies, suggested that the *Docetae* were well named, because they had a δοκὸs, or beam of timber, in their eye[1]. A more charitable philology derives their name from δοκεῖν, 'to seem.' They held that the sufferings of Christ were but seeming sufferings. As our Gospel fragment contains just the Passion and Resurrection of the Lord, we shall have ample opportunity of seeing whether it harmonizes with what we can learn of these early *Docetae.*

It is now time to come to the document itself. It was dug up six years ago in an ancient cemetery at Akhmîm (Panopolis) in Upper Egypt, and it now rests, I believe, in the Gizeh Museum at Cairo. The French Archæological Mission at Cairo have the honour of its discovery, of its identification, and of its somewhat tardy publication.

did not comprehend, this same thing ye learn from those things which are written to you,' &c.

[1] Hipp. *Ref.* viii. ad init.

The first page of the little parchment book, which contains our Gospel together with the portions of the Apocalypse and the Book of Enoch, contains no writing. It seems that the scribe had nothing but a fragment to copy from. Thus we are taken back at once, we cannot say how far, beyond the scribe himself, who is judged to have lived not earlier than the eighth century.

The second page begins:

1. "But of the Jews none washed his hands, neither Herod nor any one of His judges. And when they wished to wash them Pilate rose up. And then Herod the king commandeth that the Lord be taken[1], saying to them, What things soever I commanded you to do unto Him, do."

We begin then after the incident of Pilate washing his hands, an incident found only in S. Matthew's Gospel. Notice the use to which our writer puts it. Pilate is exonerated: the Jews must bear the blame; they cannot wash their hands. Herod's share in the Trial is mentioned only by S. Luke. Here the responsibility is shifted from Pilate's shoulders on to his. Our writer hates the Jews: his whole account is a commentary on the brief sentence of Aristides' Apology, 'He was pierced by the Jews.'

2. "And there was come there Joseph, the friend of Pilate and of the Lord; and, knowing that they were about to crucify[2] Him, he came to Pilate and asked the body of the Lord for burial. And Pilate sent to Herod and asked His body. And Herod said, Brother Pilate, even if no one had asked Him, we should have buried Him; since indeed the sabbath draweth on[3]: for it is written in the law, that

---

[1] παρ[αλημ]φθῆναι is perhaps supported by παραλαβόντες, Matt. xxiv. 27.   [2] I know no other instance of σταυρίσκειν.

[3] Cf. Jn. xix. 31, where Syr. Pesch. reads: 'They say, These bodies shall not remain on the cross, because the sabbath dawneth.'

the sun go not down on him that is put to death, on the day before the unleavened bread."

Here is a strange perversion in the narrative. Joseph is made to come to Pilate before the Crucifixion. This is explained when we observe the anxiety displayed throughout this document lest the sun should set before the burial took place. According to our writer Herod has assumed responsibility, and so the body must be asked from him. This would mean further delay, if the request be put off till the hour of the Death. We have here incidentally two details helping to exculpate Pilate: Joseph is his 'friend'; Pilate can do nothing without Herod's leave.

"The sabbath draweth on": literally 'dawneth': an expression in S. Luke xxiii. 54, where the commentators explain that the Jewish sabbath 'dawned' when Friday's sun was setting. 'Let not the sun go down upon your wrath' is S. Paul's command in Eph. iv. 26. This may illustrate the form of the command: the substance of it is in Deut. xxi. 23 (cf. Josh. x. 27), but it there applies to all days alike.

3. "And they took the Lord and pushed Him as they ran, and said, Let us drag away[1] the Son of God, having obtained power over Him. And they clothed Him with purple, and set Him on the seat of judgement, saying, Judge righteously, O king of Israel. And one of them brought a crown of thorns and put it on the head of the Lord. And others stood and spat in His eyes, and others smote His cheeks: others pricked Him with a reed; and some scourged Him, saying, With this honour let us honour the Son of God."

[1] Mr Rendel Harris suggests CYPWMEN for EYPWMEN, from Justin *Ap.* i. 35, διασύροντες. Cf. too the cry in Acts of Philip (Tisch. p. 143), Σύρατε τοὺς μάγους τούτους (just before the cod. has εὐρόντες for σύροντες). Ἄρωμεν would have the support of Isa. iii. 10, Ἄρωμεν τὸν δίκαιον, as Justin read it (*Tryph.* 137).

R. J.   2

For the illustration of this passage we turn to Justin Martyr (*Apol.* i. 35): 'For, as the prophet said, they dragged Him and set Him on the judgement seat, and said, Judge for us[1].' This depends on Isa. lviii. 2, quoted by Justin just before: 'They ask of me judgement, and dare to draw nigh to God.' The Septuagint Version (and indeed the Hebrew text) has, 'They ask of me just judgement,' which is still closer to our Gospel. But whence came to Justin or to our author the conception that the Lord was set upon the judgement seat? Whence, but from the Gospel of S. John? There we read: 'When Pilate therefore heard these words, he brought Jesus out, and sat upon the judgement seat[2].' But Archbishop Whately used to translate the words, 'and set Him on the judgement seat'—a perfectly legitimate rendering of the Greek. So it seems Justin Martyr read them: and so too the writer of our Gospel, or the source from which he borrowed.

4. "And they brought two malefactors, and they crucified the Lord between them. But He held His peace, as having no pain. And when they had raised the cross they wrote upon it, This is the king of Israel. And having set His garments before Him they parted them among them, and cast a lot[3] for them. And one of those malefactors reproached them, saying, We have suffered thus for the evils that we have done, but this man, having become the Saviour of men, what wrong hath He done to you? And they, being angered at him, commanded that his legs should not be broken, that he might die in torment."

---

[1] Διασύροντες αὐτὸν ἐκάθισαν ἐπὶ τοῦ βήματος καὶ εἶπον Κρῖνον ἡμῖν.

[2] Jn. xix. 13 καὶ ἐκάθισεν ἐπὶ βήματος. Cf. Salmon, *Introd. to N. T.* ed. 4. p. 74 n.

[3] Λαχμὸν ἔβαλον. The word λαχμὸς is a rare one: the earliest authority seems to be Justin, who uses it in this connection, *Tryph.* 97.

' He held His peace, as having no pain ' is our first sign
that this is the Gospel of the *Docetae*. Observe that, to
make room for this, the words ' Father, forgive them ; for
they know not what they do ' must be omitted. Our writer
is no friend of the Jews : he would willingly omit a prayer
for their forgiveness. But it is worthy of notice that the
words in question, which are found only in S. Luke xxiii.
34, are omitted there by some very important MSS.[1], and
may not have been present in our author's copy of S. Luke.

Note here, too, one of the many strange perversions in
this Gospel : in S. Luke one malefactor chides the other :
here the reproach is addressed to the Jews. Again, ' the
breaking of the legs ' is strangely perverted : but it is
another echo of S. John.

5. . "And it was noon, and darkness covered all Judæa :
and they were troubled and distressed, lest the sun had
gone down, since He yet lived : [for] it was written for
them, that the sun go not down on him that is put to death.
And one of them said, Give Him to drink gall with vinegar.
And they mixed and gave Him to drink, and fulfilled all
things, and accomplished their sins against their own head."

' Fulfilled all things ' takes us again to S. John (xix. 28):
' Jesus, knowing that all things were already finished, that
the Scripture might be accomplished (a respectable number
of MSS., headed by Codex Sinaiticus, reads ' fulfilled '),
said, I thirst...they set on hyssop a sponge full of vinegar '
(again a respectable group of MSS. adds ' with gall '). This
last addition is clearly based on Ps. lxix. 21, ' They gave
me gall for my meat ; and in my thirst they gave me
vinegar to drink.' S. Matthew also mentions ' wine mingled

---

[1] E.g. the Vatican MS., the Codex Bezae at Cambridge, and an
early corrector of the Sinaitic Codex.

with gall' (xxvii. 34) ; but that is before crucifixion, and is his version, based upon the Psalm, of words which S. Mark preserves to us more precisely as 'myrrhed wine,' offered to lull the pain and refused by the Lord. It seems as though the draught here given was intended to hasten death.

If there is one word in the Canonical narratives of the Passion which is calculated to set our minds at rest on the question whether our Blessed Lord truly felt the pain of Crucifixion, it is the word from the Cross, 'I thirst.' During the hours of darkness it would seem that a great spiritual struggle was taking place, and this is marked by the quotation of the first verse of the twenty-second Psalm. At its close the tortured body for a moment claims and receives attention ; and the cry of thirst is heard from the parched lips of the Sufferer. The value of this word to us receives fresh illustration from the fact that it can find no place in a Docetic Gospel, although the writer uses words which come before and after it in S. John's narrative.

"And many went about with lamps, supposing that it was night, and fell down[1]. And the Lord cried out, saying, My power, My power, thou hast forsaken Me. And when He had said it He was taken up. And in that hour the vail of the temple of Jerusalem was rent in twain[2]."

[1] In a document purporting to be an account of the Crucifixion sent by Pilate to the Emperor Tiberius, Pilate is made to say that not even the Emperor could be ignorant 'that in all the world they lighted lamps from the sixth hour until evening': *Anaphora Pilati*, B. c. 7 (Tisch. *Evv. Apocr.* ed. 2 p. 446 f.). For ἐπέσαντο, at the end of the sentence, I have written ἔπεσάν τε: cf. Isa. lix. 10 καὶ πεσοῦνται ἐν μεσημβρίᾳ ὡς ἐν μεσονυκτίῳ. It also seems an echo of Jn. xviii. 3, 6 ἔρχεται μετὰ φανῶν καὶ λαμπάδων...καὶ ἔπεσαν χαμαί.

[2] For αὐτὸς ὥρας we must read αὐτῆς ὥρας, or perhaps αὐτῆς τῆς ὥρας: αὐτὴ is the equivalent in later Greek literature of ἐκείνη (as in the modern tongue); cf. Lc. x. 7, 21, and xii. 12 (|| ἐκείνῃ Mt. Mc.).

This is the most startling passage in the document. The view that underlies it is that the Divine Christ came down upon the Human Christ at the Baptism in the form of a Dove, and departed from the Human Christ upon the Cross. Irenæus, a contemporary of Serapion, denounces the doctrine 'that one Christ suffered and rose again, and another flew up and remained free from suffering[1].'

'The power' then, so often emphasised in S. Luke's Gospel in connection with the person of our Lord[2], is here, by a strange perversion of our Lord's quotation from Ps. xxii. 1, described as forsaking Him: the Divine Christ is 'taken up,' the Human Christ remains upon the Cross. *Eli, Eli* is rendered as 'My power, My power[3].' We are thus confirmed in the belief that this was the Gospel, as Serapion tells us, of the *Docetae*[4].

---

[1] Iren. III. 12. 2, where he seems to have Cerinthus specially in mind, cf. III. 11. 1. Compare too his description of the Valentinian doctrine in I. 7. 2.

[2] Compare especially Lc. i. 35 'the power of the Most High shall overshadow thee,' iv. 14 'in the power of the Spirit,' v. 17 'the power of the Lord was present that He should heal,' vi. 19 'power came forth from Him and healed them all'; also viii. 46 (∥ Mc. v. 30) : and note besides Lc. xxiv. 49; Acts i. 8, viii. 10.

[3] Eusebius, in an interesting note upon the Psalm (*Dem. Ev.* x. 8, p. 494), tells us that Aquila, who strove to give a more literal translation than the LXX, rendered the words ' My strong one, My strong one' (ἰσχυρέ μου, ἰσχυρέ μου), but that the exact meaning was 'My strength, My strength' (ἰσχύς μου, ἰσχύς μου). The rendering in our text must be added to the list of authorities that support the form *Eli*, as against *Eloi*, in the New Testament. In interpreting 'Israel' Justin (*Tryph.* 125) says: τὸ δὲ ἠλ δύναμις.

[4] For the use of the text in question among the Valentinians, cf. Iren. I. 8. 2. We must distinguish these early *Docetae* from the later heretics, who denied the reality of Christ's body: see Dr Salmon's articles *Docetae* and *Docetism* in *Dict. Christ. Biogr.*

6. "And then they drew out the nails from the hands of the Lord, and laid Him upon the earth, and the earth all quaked, and great fear arose. Then the sun shone, and it was found the ninth hour: and the Jews rejoiced, and gave His body to Joseph that he might bury it, since he had seen what good things He had done. And he took the Lord, and washed Him, and rolled Him in a linen cloth, and brought Him into his own tomb, which was called the Garden of Joseph."

Here again we have echoes of S. John. He alone mentions the Nails[1]: he alone mentions the Garden.

The Jews rejoiced, when the sun shone out again, because they found that it was only the ninth hour, and not sunset: so that the law might still be complied with.

7. "Then the Jews and the elders and the priests, seeing what evil they had done to themselves, began to lament and to say, Woe for our sins: for the judgement and the end of Jerusalem hath drawn nigh. And I with my companions was grieved; and being wounded in mind we hid ourselves: for we were being sought for by them as malefactors, and as wishing to set fire to the temple. And upon all these things we fasted and sat mourning and weeping night and day until the sabbath."

The cry of Woe is found in Tatian's Diatessaron, a Gospel Harmony made about the middle of the second century and chiefly known to us through an Armenian version of S. Ephrem's Syriac Commentary upon it. Thus

---

[1] It is curious that neither here nor in Jn. xx. 25, 27 is there any reference to Nails through the Feet. In the *Anaphora Pilati*, B. 7, one MS. reads: 'And there began to be earthquakes in the hour in which the nails were fixed in the hands and feet of Jesus, until the evening." Here, however, the earthquake is placed later than in S. Matthew, who alone mentions it.

we read[1]: 'Woe was it, Woe was it unto us: this was the Son of God: ...the judgements of the desolation of Jerusalem have come.' The Old Syriac Version adds to Lc. xxiii. 48, 'Woe to us: what hath befallen us? Woe to us from our sins.' And one Latin Codex (S. Germanensis, g₁) has: 'Woe to us: what hath happened this day for our sins? for the desolation of Jerusalem hath drawn nigh[2].'

8. " But the scribes and Pharisees and elders being gathered together one with another, when they heard that all the people murmured and beat their breasts saying, If by His death these most mighty signs have come to pass, see how just He is,—the elders were afraid and came to Pilate, beseeching him and saying, Give us soldiers, that they may watch His sepulchre for three days, lest His disciples come and steal Him away, and the people suppose that He is risen from the dead and do us evil. And Pilate gave them Petronius the centurion with soldiers to watch the tomb. And the elders and scribes came with them to the sepulchre, and having rolled a great stone together with[3] the centurion and the soldiers they all together who were there set it at the door of the sepulchre; and they put upon it seven seals, and they pitched a tent there and kept watch."

Longinus is the name of the centurion at the Cross in the 'Acts of Pilate.' It is of course not necessary to identify the two centurions: but we shall see presently that the words attributed in our Gospels to the centurion

---

[1] Eph. *Diat.* p. 224 (Moesinger pp. 245 f., cf. p. 248). The word for ' desolation ' is that used for ἐρήμωσις in the Armenian Gospels.

[2] Vae nobis, quae facta sunt hodie propter peccata nostra: appropinquauit enim desolatio Hierusalem.

[3] The text is here corrupt: for it says that 'they rolled the stone *upon* the centurion (κατὰ τοῦ κεντυρίωνος).' I have ventured to substitute μετὰ, 'together with:' cf. Mt. xxvii. 66.

at the Cross are here assigned to the centurion at the Sepulchre[1].

9. "And early in the morning as the sabbath was drawing on[2] there came a multitude from Jerusalem and the region round about, that they might see the sepulchre that was sealed. And in the night in which the Lord's day was drawing on, as the soldiers kept watch two by two on guard, there was a great voice in the heaven; and they saw the heavens opened, and two men descending thence with great light and approaching the tomb. And that stone which was put at the door rolled away of itself and departed to one side; and the tomb was opened and both the young men entered in.

10. "When therefore the soldiers saw it, they awakened the centurion and the elders, for they too were hard by keeping watch; and, as they declared what things they had seen, again they see coming forth from the tomb three men, and the two supporting the one, and a cross following them. And of the two the head reached unto the heaven, but the head of Him that was led by them overpassed the heavens. And they heard a voice from the heavens, saying, Hast thou preached to them that sleep[3]? And an answer was heard from the cross, Yea."

[1] Petronius is a disciple of S. Peter in the Acts of S. Hermione (Sept. 4).

[2] The same phrase as in § 2; ἐπιφώσκοντος τοῦ σαββάτου, and immediately afterwards ἐπέφωσκεν ἡ κυριακή; but here apparently from Mt. xxviii. 1.

[3] When a document of this kind, where the text is frequently corrupt, first comes to light, it is difficult to assign to individuals the true share of credit for emendations that sometimes arise in common: but I must mention that I owe to Mr F. C. Burkitt the suggestion that the Voice from heaven should be taken as a question. To him and to other friends I am very deeply indebted.

No subject had a greater fascination for the early Christian mind than the Descent of Christ into Hades and 'the Harrowing of Hell.' The only unmistakeable reference to it in the New Testament is in S. Peter's First Epistle (1 Pet. iii. 19, iv. 6), 'He went and preached to the spirits in prison,' and 'The gospel was preached to the dead.' But it is also possible that the ancient hymn, from which S. Paul quotes in Eph. v. 14, 'Wherefore it saith,

Awake, thou that sleepest,
And arise from the dead,
And Christ shall shine upon thee,'

was intended to represent the triumph-song with which the Lord entered the Under-world.

In seeking the source of the actual words of the Voice from heaven, we may note that S. Matthew says that at the moment of Christ's Death, 'many bodies of the saints that had fallen asleep arose' (xxvii. 52). But we must also compare a passage which Justin Martyr says the Jews cut out from the prophecy of Jeremiah in their copies of the LXX.: 'The Lord God, the Holy One of Israel, remembered His dead that had fallen asleep aforetime in the earth of burial, and descended to them to proclaim to them the good news of His salvation [1].' Irenaeus also quotes this passage several times: but we have no reason to believe that it ever formed part of the Old Testament Scriptures. But yet it is important, if only to shew how much these thoughts were in the air in early times: a fact to which further witness is borne by the Gospel of Nicodemus [2], an apocryphal work

---

[1] See Bp. Lightfoot's note on Ign. *Magn.* ix. I read with Irenaeus προκεκοιμημένων. This is supported also by Hermas, who says of the Apostles (*Sim.* ix. 16, 5) κοιμηθέντες...ἐκήρυξαν καὶ τοῖς προκεκοιμημένοις.

[2] In the Gospel of Nicodemus II. 10 (Tisch. p. 430), the Cross is

containing a full description of the Descent into Hell, and by the Anaphora of Pilate, to which reference has been already made. A few sentences of this last book are worth quoting here, as their thoughts are closely akin to those of our document. 'And on the first day of the week, about the third hour of the night, the sun was seen as never it had shone before, and all the heaven was brightened. And even as lightnings come in a storm, so certain men of lofty stature, in adornment of apparel and of glory indescribable, appeared in the air, and a multitude of angels crying aloud and saying, Glory in the highest to God, and upon earth peace, among men good will: come up out of Hades, ye that have been enslaved in the under-world of Hades[1].'

In a heretical book called 'the Wanderings of the Apostles,' which Dr Zahn says[2] 'must have been written

left in the Under-world: 'and the Lord placed His Cross in the midst of Hell (in medio inferni), which is the sign of victory and shall remain there even for evermore.'

[1] *Anaph. Pil.*, B. 8 (Tisch. p. 447). This book has clearly some close connection with our document. Beside the striking resemblances already cited, we may note that Pilate makes Herod and the Jews responsible for the Death of Christ; and, whereas here the disciples were supposed to wish to set fire to the Temple, there all the Synagogues in Jerusalem save one are swallowed up in the earthquake. A small coincidence of language is found in A. 10 (Tisch. 441) ἦν θεασάμενος, cf. supra § 6. We may even wonder whether the earlier part of the Anaphora does not preserve details from the still missing part of our Gospel: e.g. there is the same use of S. John, and the same strange perversion, in the account of Lazarus, who is said to have been in an advanced state of corruption, and yet to have come forth from the tomb like a bridegroom from his chamber.

[2] Zahn *Acta Johannis* p. cxliv. On p. 216 he gives the passage of Photius, *Cod.* 114, on these Leucian Acts, which I have cited here.

Hermas *Sim.* ix. 6, 1 introduces the Lord as 'a Man of lofty stature, so as to overtop the tower': and in S. Perpetua's Vision (*Passio* x.) He is represented as 'a Man of marvellous greatness, so

before 160,' and of which fragments are preserved to us, we are told that Christ appeared in various forms to His disciples, sometimes as a young man, then as an old man, then again as a boy; and sometimes small, and sometimes 'very large, so that at times His head reached even unto heaven.' Further coincidences tend to shew that this book too stands in some near relation to our Gospel.

11. "They therefore considered one with another whether to go away and shew these things to Pilate. And while they yet thought thereon the heavens again appear opened, and a certain man descending and entering into the sepulchre. When the centurion and they that were with him saw these things, they hastened by night to Pilate, leaving the tomb which they were watching, and declared all things which they had seen, being distressed and saying, Truly He was the Son of God. Pilate answered and said, I am pure from the blood of the Son of God: but ye determined this. Then they all drew near and besought him and entreated him to command the centurion and the soldiers to say nothing of the things which they had seen: For it is better, say they, for us to owe the greatest debt of sin before God, and not to fall into the hand of the people of the Jews and to be stoned. Pilate therefore commanded the centurion and the soldiers to say nothing."

The hatred of the writer to the Jews, which stands in striking contrast to the just and measured terms of our Evangelists, is nowhere more marked than in the keen satire

as to overpass the top of the amphitheatre.' With reference to the two men who support the Lord it is interesting to note a representation in early art, in which 'our Lord in glory stands by and supports a large cross, having the angels Michael and Gabriel on either hand.' *Dict. Christ. Antiqq.* vol. I. p. 497. Michael and Gabriel come for the soul of B.V. Mary in *Transitus Mariae* B. 8 (Tisch. p. 130).

of this passage. Pilate once more is freed as far as possible from blame[1].

12. "And at dawn upon the Lord's day Mary Magdalen, a disciple of the Lord, [who] fearing because of the Jews, since they were burning with wrath, had not done at the Lord's sepulchre the things which the women are wont to do for those that die and that are beloved by them, took her friends with her and came to the sepulchre where He was laid. And they feared lest the Jews should see them, and they said, Even if on that day on which He was crucified we could not weep and lament, yet now let us do these things at His sepulchre. But who shall roll away for us the stone that is laid at the door of the sepulchre, that we may enter in and sit by Him and do the things that are due? For the stone was great, and we fear lest some one see us. And even if we cannot, yet let us set at the door the things which we bring for a memorial of Him; let us weep and lament, until we come unto our home.

13. "And they went away and found the tomb opened, and coming near they looked in there ; and they see there a certain young man sitting in the midst of the tomb, beautiful and clothed in a very bright robe; who said to them, Why are ye come? whom seek ye? Is it that crucified One? He is risen and gone away. But if ye believe not, look in and see the place where He lay, that He is not [here][2]; for

---

[1] The white-washing of the unhappy Roman governor was some-times carried further still. In the *Paradosis Pilati* (Tisch. p. 455) in answer to Pilate's prayer for forgiveness before his execution by Tiberius a voice comes from heaven saying, 'All generations shall call thee blessed...for under thee all these things were fulfilled': and an angel of the Lord receives his head.

[2] In Lc. xxiv. 6 we have 'non est, surrexit' in Cod. Sangerm. (g₂): and perhaps we ought not to add 'here' in this place.

He is risen and gone away thither, whence He was sent[1]. Then the women feared and fled."

This passage, which opens with clear traces of S. John, (compare especially xix. 40, 'as the custom of the Jews is to bury'), is also full of the peculiar phrases of S. Mark. The correspondence ends too with the abrupt conclusion of S. Mark's Gospel, as we now have it: and there is no trace of the twelve disputed verses[2].

13. "Now it was the last day of the unleavened bread, and many went forth returning to their homes, as the feast was ended. But we, the twelve[3] disciples of the Lord, mourned and were grieved: and each one grieving for that which was come to pass departed to his home. But I Simon Peter and Andrew my brother took our nets and went away to the sea; and there was with us Levi the son of Alphaeus, whom the Lord...."

[1] With this we must compare the 20th Homily of Aphrahat (ed. Wright, p. 385), 'And the angel said to Mary, He is risen and gone away to Him that sent Him' (cf. Jn. xvi. 5). There is reason to believe that Aphrahat, a Syrian writer, used Tatian's Harmony: and thus we seem to have a second link between our Gospel and that important work.

Whatever be the origin of the addition, it is in direct contrast to Jn. xx. 17, 'I am not yet ascended to the Father.' In our Book however the Ascension of both Christs has taken place already.

[2] Cf. in Mc. xvi. 3 ff. τίς ἀποκυλίσει ἡμῖν...ἦν γὰρ μέγας...νεανίσκον καθημένον...περιβεβλημένον στολήν: and compare the last words ἔφυγον ...ἐφοβοῦντο γάρ with this document φοβηθεῖσαι ἔφυγον. Here as in S. Mark there is no record of an appearance of the Lord to the women.

[3] 'The twelve disciples' is perhaps a mere slip of the author or of a copyist: but it is conceivable that Judas too as well as Pilate underwent a cleansing process, if indeed he was ever mentioned, in our writer's narrative. The reading 'twelve' is confirmed by the Apocalypse (§ 2) which has the same phrase, 'we the twelve disciples.'

This broken sentence must remain unfinished, till some new discovery tells us what we long to know—whether in this Gospel the Disciples ever see the Lord.   Meanwhile we may be grateful that it adds a final proof of what indeed is clear enough already to a reader of the original Greek, namely our writer's use of the Fourth Gospel.   It is probable enough that if we knew what followed we should find that he 'had honoured it with the honour' which he has given to it already with the same impartiality as to the other three— the honour of misrepresentation.   Perversion is a form of witness to the thing perverted.

Now that we have read our new Gospel, what are we to think of it?

The document will doubtless be subjected to the most searching criticism both in England and elsewhere, and it would be presumptuous to pretend to give the final verdict. But a few general remarks may not be out of place at the close of this Lecture.

And, first, I would call attention to the fact that all our most recent recoveries are not entire surprises.   Nothing wholly new and unheard of turns up as we explore neglected libraries or dig in disused cemeteries.   The range of Christian literature in the second century was limited.   Eusebius, to whose researches we owe a debt of gratitude which can never be too generously acknowledged, covered it practically all by his own reading or by the reports of others. It is true that, now that we have entered upon a new field of exploration in the tombs of Egypt, there is nothing that we need despair of finding—be it the Expositions of Papias, or the Memoirs of Hegesippus, or the Chronicle of Julius Africanus.   But again and again our new friend has proved to be an old one, whom we knew at least by name. And he has fitted in at once into the old surroundings. The second century was a book-making age; but the books were very often not original. As Spurgeon used to say of many modern books, 'They stir up our pure minds by way of remembrance.' Books were made out of books. The literary imagination played around the old facts or the old records. The Teaching of the Apostles used an earlier, perhaps a Jewish, manual: the Apology of Aristides was indebted to a book still unrecovered, the Preaching of Peter. Each of these in turn was embodied in later works: the Teaching was 'used and used up,' as we are told, in the Shepherd of Hermas, besides the more obvious places where we trace it: the Apology of Aristides lies embedded in a religious novel. Similarly, there can be no manner of doubt as to whence our new Gospel derived the main bulk of its facts and of its language. But as it was a true 'Apocryphon,' the secret book of a sect and not the common property of the Catholic Church, its circulation was but limited and we cannot expect to find it largely used in the later writings which have come down to us. Indeed it is surprising that it should have so many points of contact as we have already noted with the surrounding literature.

The second point to which I would call attention is a very different one. We are sometimes told that certain of the Books of the New Testament are *Tendenz-schriften*: that is to say, they are composed with the aim of setting forth at any cost the peculiar view of some special school of Christian thought. Well, here we have a good example of a 'Tendency-Writing.' It is worth careful study from this point of view. Old statements are suppressed, or wilfully perverted and displaced: new statements are introduced which bear their condemnation on their faces. No-

thing is left as it was before.   Here is 'History as it should
be': 'Lines left out' of the old familiar records.   And no
one who will take the pains to compare sentence by sentence, word by word, the new 'Lines left out' with the old
'Line upon Line,' will fail to return to the Four Gospels
with a sense of relief at his escape from a stifling prison of
prejudice into the transparent and the bracing atmosphere
of pure simplicity and undesigning candour.

Thirdly, I must try to say a word about the date of our
new Book.   The points in which our writer seems to coin-
cide with Tatian, together with the use of the Four Gospels
side by side, suggesting that the work is based upon a
previous Harmony, might make us hesitate to place it
earlier than *c.* 170.   But on the other hand its seeming
coincidence with the Leucian Acts, which deserves a full
investigation, tends to push it back before 160.   For the
whole style of the narrative is much less complex, and
indeed suggests at once a very early date.   In all the
instances of similarity with other books we cannot prove as
yet that our author has borrowed, save from the Four
Gospels.   In every other case he may have used some
source used also by the other writers and now entirely lost :
nay, in some cases he may be the original authority himself.   The main views here expounded may be traced back
even to Cerinthus the opponent of S. John : and we know
that S. Ignatius strenuously combated Docetic teachers.
So that we need not be surprised if further evidence shall
tend to place this Gospel nearer to the beginning than to
the middle of the second century.

Lastly, the unmistakeable acquaintance of the author
with our Four Evangelists deserves a special comment[1].   He

[1] In the margin of the Greek text I have placed references *only* to
those lines in which some statement or phrase occurs which is *peculiar*

uses and misuses each in turn. To him they all stand on an equal footing. He lends no support to the attempt which has been made to place a gulf of separation between the Fourth Gospel and the rest, as regards the period or area of their acceptance as Canonical. Nor again does he countenance the theory of the continued circulation in the second century of an *Urevangelium*, or such a prae-canonical Gospel as we feel must lie behind our Synoptists. He uses our Greek Gospels; there is no proof (though the possibility of course is always open) that he knew of any Gospel record other than these.

And so the new facts are just what they should be, if the Church's universal tradition as to the supreme and unique position of the Four Canonical Gospels is still to be sustained by historical criticism. The words of Irenaeus (III. 11. 7), as the second century was drawing to a close, are as true as ever to-day, and they have received a new and notable confirmation by our latest recovery:

'So strong is the position of our Gospels, that the heretics themselves bear witness to them, and each must start from these to prove his own doctrine....Since therefore those who contradict us lend us their testimony and use our Gospels, the claim which we have made on their behalf is thereby confirmed and verified.'

to one of our Four Gospels. Thus the use made of the distinctive parts of each Gospel may be seen at a glance.

ADDITIONAL NOTES.

·1. ON § 5 AND CODEX BOBBIENSIS. It seems as though we had at last a parallel to the extraordinary interpolation at Mc. xvi. 4 in cod. Bobbiensis (k), an Old Latin MS., which reads, after 'Who shall roll away for us the stone from the door,' as follows instead of our verse 4: 'But suddenly, at the third hour of the day, darkness came over the whole world, and angels descended from heaven, and rising in the glory of the living God ascended with Him; and immediately it became light.' This passage clearly cannot belong to its present context: but it closely corresponds with the Ascension of the Divine Christ from the Cross; even to the mention of the reappearance of the sun. The 'hour' may have been changed, so as to be less inconsistent when the passage had got into its new context.

2. ON THE CHRONOLOGY OF THIS GOSPEL. The notes of time are as follows:

1. σάββατον ἐπιφώσκει...πρὸ μιᾶς τῶν ἀζύμων. The Body must not remain unburied after sunset on this day.

2. ἦν δὲ μεσημβρία. The darkness covers Judaea.

3. εὑρέθη ὥρα ἐνάτη. The light returns.

4. νυκτὸς καὶ ἡμέρας ἕως τοῦ σαββάτου. The Disciples fast and mourn.

5. ἐπὶ τρεῖς ἡμέρας. The Jews propose to watch the Tomb.

6. πρωΐας δὲ ἐπιφώσκοντος τοῦ σαββάτου. The multitude come to see the Tomb.

7. τῇ δὲ νυκτὶ ᾗ ἐπέφωσκεν ἡ κυριακή. The Voice and the Vision.

8. νυκτός. They hasten to tell Pilate.

9. ὄρθρου δὲ τῆς κυριακῆς. Mary Magdalen comes to the Tomb with the other women.

10. ἦν δὲ τελευταία ἡμέρα τῶν ἀζύμων...τῆς ἑορτῆς παυσαμένης. Many return to their homes. The Disciples go to the sea.

We may perhaps arrange them in order thus:

Abib 14.	Preparation	1, 2, 3,
	At even Passover killed. Period of unleavened bread begins.	
15.	Sabbath. Sheaf waved	[4], 6
16.	First day of the week	5, 7, 8, 9
17.	Second „ „	
18.	Third „ „	
19.	Fourth „ „	
20.	Fifth „ „	
21.	Preparation	10
	At even Period of unleavened bread ends.	
22.	Sabbath	[4]

In § 13 the Disciples are still 'weeping and mourning': so that we may explain 4 perhaps as meaning all the days until the second sabbath. In fact a *u*-shaped β may have fallen out after τοῦ: so that we might possibly restore τοῦ β' σαββάτου. But this is not necessary, as the first sabbath had begun at the time referred to. It is remarkable then that the Disciples remain a week in hiding at Jerusalem, and then leave it for Galilee without having seen the Lord at all. The first of these statements may be suggested by Jn. xx. 26; but the second, while it might be suggested by the silence of S. Matthew and S. Mark, is in direct contrast with Lc. xxiv. 34, 36 and Jn. xx. 19, 26.

3. ON THE RECONSTRUCTION OF THIS GOSPEL. I have already suggested (pp. 20, 22, 26) that the *Anaphora Pilati* has used this Gospel: and this view is confirmed by some Coptic fragments (Revillout, 1876), as yet untranslated, my knowledge of which is gained from Mr James. In these the same stress is laid on the corruption of the body of Lazarus; and Philip appears together with Herod as plotting against the Lord, as in *Anaph. Pil.* Moreover these fragments seem to be connected in method with others which correspond to the *Historia Josephi*, in which we find the one statement which Origen preserves to us from this Gospel (see above p. 14 n.) set forth in full.

THE REVELATION OF PETER

A LECTURE

ON THE NEWLY RECOVERED FRAGMENT

BY

MONTAGUE RHODES JAMES M.A.

ET APPAREBIT LACVS TORMENTI ET CONTRA
ILLVM ERIT LOCVS REQVIETIONIS: ET CLIBANVS
GEHENNAE OSTENDETVR ET CONTRA EVM IOCVN-
DITATIS PARADISVS

THE REVELATION OF PETER.

OF the two fragments of early Christian literature which have just been called out of Egypt, the extract from the Gospel of Peter is no doubt the more immediately interesting: and, in the excitement caused by that, the Apocalyptic fragment, which follows it in the Gizeh MS., runs some chance of being overlooked. And yet, had this latter stood by itself, its discovery would have caused a very considerable stir in the theological world. No one interested in the history of the Canon of the New Testament could have failed to be excited when nearly half of the text of the Revelation of Peter was laid before him.

For this book was one of which we heard much and saw very little. It always seemed strange that we were constantly encountering its name in early documents, and yet, when we came to inquire about its character and contents, there were exactly six passages which gave us any idea on the subject, while the total amount of the text which they preserved may have been eight lines. Curiously enough, moreover, modern writers on the subject had hardly ventured more than the most general conjectures on these fragments, and had not succeeded in drawing from them by any means all the information which, scanty as they were, they could be made to afford.

For myself, they had always possessed a curious interest, as being the remains of a book once highly prized in several important Christian communities, and, more than that, as being the relics of the earliest Christian Apocalypse, save one, that was ever written: and, in the year 1886, I had taken some pains in collecting and commenting on these poor relics, and, in particular, in attempting to reconstruct by their aid the probable contents of the book, and to estimate its influence on later works of the same class.

In the course of these investigations it became clear that the book must have contained at least two elements, one a prophetical or predictive section, relating to the end of the world, the other, a narrative of visions; and more particularly, a vision of the torments of the wicked, in which various classes of sinners were represented as punished in a manner suitable to their offences. It became clear, moreover, that certain books showed more or less clear traces of obligation to this old Apocalypse: in particular, this was true of the second book of the Sibylline oracles, the Apocalypse of Paul, and the later Apocalypse of Esdras. And,—what was interesting from the literary point of view,—we could trace the influence of the Apocalypse of Paul upon almost all the mediaeval visions, even in the *Divina Commedia* of Dante. So that through the medium of the Pauline vision, the Apocalypse of Peter had had a share in moulding the greatest poem of the middle ages. In my recent edition of the Testament of Abraham[1] I took occasion to set forth the main lines of this view: but it was not possible there (nor will it be, I fear, on the present occasion) to set forth, with all the necessary detail, the steps which led me to the conclusions which I have just stated. But perhaps I have said enough to

[1] *Texts and Studies*, ii. 2, pp. 23, 24.

show that the Apocalypse of Peter had for some time occupied no small share of my attention; and I hope this will justify the precipitation with which I have ventured to attack the newly-discovered fragment.

It is time, however, to leave generalities and to approach details. I propose to divide this paper into three heads—a practice for which I fancy there are precedents. Under the first I shall arrange my account of what was known about the book previous to this late discovery. Under the second I shall give a translation of the new fragment, with a few notes. Under the third I shall try to state what new light this discovery throws upon the book as a whole.

It is perhaps simplest to tell the story of our book in the words of the writers who speak of it, arranging them in order of date. The first mention (real or apparent) of an Apocalypse of Peter is found in the Muratorian Fragment, dated *circ.* 170—200 A.D. The writer has mentioned the Wisdom of Solomon: he goes on to say: "The Apocalypses of John and Peter only do we receive: which (in the singular) some of our number will not have read in the churches." Most critics have understood this sentence to mean that the only Apocalypses (and the number of Apocalypses was large) which the Roman Church received were those of John and Peter; and that the *latter* was repudiated by some Roman Christians. But it has been lately urged with great ingenuity by Dr Zahn, that there is no reason to believe that the Petrine Apocalypse was known at all at Rome; and that we ought to suppose that a line has here dropped out of our undoubtedly corrupt fragment, and to read: "(There is) the Apocalypse of John and of Peter *one epistle, which* alone we receive: *there is also a second (epistle),* which some of our number will not have read in church[1]."

[1] Zahn, *N. T. Kanon,* ii. 105 sqq.

I do not feel convinced that Dr Zahn is right, more particularly as it seems that we have some reason to believe that Hippolytus used our book.

Of Clement of Alexandria, at the beginning of the third century, Eusebius tells us[1] that in his great lost work, the *Hypotyposes* or *Outlines*, he commented on all the Canonical Scripture, 'not even omitting the disputed scriptures, I mean the Epistle of Jude and the rest of the Catholic Epistles, and that of Barnabas, and the so-called Apocalypse of Peter.'

When we turn to Clement's works, in the collection of extracts (either from a lost book of his *Miscellanies*, or from the *Outlines*) which are called *Eclogae ex Scripturis Propheticis*, we find three separate quotations (and a fourth passage repeating one of the three) from this Apocalypse[2], in one of which it is called 'the Scripture.'

I shall reserve for the present the translation of these fragments.

S. Methodius of Olympus in Lycia, living at the end of the third century, has a fairly long passage identical in part with one of the Clementine quotations; and the material of this passage is taken, he says, from 'divinely-inspired writings[3].'

So far, then, Lycia, Alexandria, and probably Rome, are witnesses to the early popularity of the Apocalypse.

In the fourth century we have a *critical* estimate of the book,—where we naturally expect to find it,—in the *Ecclesiastical History* of Eusebius of Caesarea. Twice over he gives us his view of the book, based largely on the use or non-use of it by earlier Church writers: and it is by no means a favourable view.

[1] *H. E.* vi. 14, 1.   [2] See Fragments 3—6.
[3] See Fragment 5 *b*.

In the former of the two passages he enumerates the writings, genuine and spurious, which were current under the name of S. Peter; of the spurious writings he says: "the book, so entitled, of his *Acts*, and the so-called *Gospel* according to him, and what is known as his *Preaching*, and what is called his *Apocalypse*—these we know not at all as having been handed down among catholic scriptures; for no ancient Church writer, nor contemporary of our own, has made use of testimonies taken from them[1]." As a matter of fact, we know that Clement of Alexandria used both *Preaching* and *Apocalypse*: still, in its broad lines, the statement is no doubt correct.

The second of Eusebius's estimates of this book is to be found in his famous classification of the New Testament writings[2]. The place assigned to it is below the limbo of disputed books, but in the uppermost circle of the abode of spurious ones, among those which, though certainly spurious, or outside the pale, were not of distinctly heretical tendencies. 'Among spurious books let there be classed: the writing of the *Acts of Paul*, and the book called the *Shepherd*, and the *Apocalypse of Peter*, and, besides these, the *Epistle of Barnabas*, and what are called the *Teachings of the Apostles*: and besides, if you take that view, as I said above, the *Apocalypse of John*...and some include in this class the *Gospel according to the Hebrews*. All these will be of the number of *disputed* books.' So that Eusebius himself applies to this class both the terms *spurious* and *disputed*: but I think the former more truly represents his own opinion, and the softening down of it is a concession to the opinions of many of his contemporaries.

Macarius Magnes, a writer of the beginning of the fifth century, furnishes us with two more fragments of our book.

[1] *H. E.* iii. 3, 2.　　[2] *H. E.* iii. 25, 4.

The nature of his evidence requires a word of explanation. His book, called *Apocritica*, gives a series of objections brought by a heathen against Christianity, and the answers to these by Macarius. Now the objections are evidently genuine, and seem to be taken out of a written work. And it is thought very likely that the author of them may be Porphyry. In that case, the quotations must be set down as a testimony to the currency of our book in the *third* century. The heathen objector adduces the book 'by way of superfluity,' apparently not attaching much importance to it. Macarius, when he comes to explain the matter, takes no pains to defend the source of the quotation : 'Even if we repudiate the Apocalypse of Peter, we are forced by the utterances of prophecy and of the Gospel, to agree with the Apocalypse of Peter.'

More light on the reception of the book is given us by Sozomen in the first half of the fifth century. 'For instance,' he says, 'the so-called Apocalypse of Peter, which was stamped as entirely spurious by the ancients, we have discovered to be read in certain churches of Palestine up to the present day, once a year, on the Friday during which the people most religiously fast in commemoration of the Lord's passion[1].'

This exhausts the list of *notices* of the book : it is true that Rufinus in his version of Eusebius retains the Apocalypse of Peter (in *H. E.* VI. 14) and omits the Catholic Epistles: but this is because Eusebius calls the latter *disputed* in that place.

Jerome, again, merely translates Eusebius (*H. E.* III. 3) when he enumerates the works attributed to Peter: Nicephorus, too, copies Eusebius and Sozomen.

---

[1] *Hist. Eccl.* vii. 19.

But a certain amount of evidence remains : we have three lists of apocryphal books which mention our Apocalypse. The list which goes by the name of Nicephorus, and may be placed about 850 A.D., is interesting as containing the name we are in search of, and as being a production of some one writing at Jerusalem[1]. One division of this list is set apart for 'disputed books of the New Testament.' These are :

The Apocalypse of John	containing 1400 lines.
The Apocalypse of Peter	.... 300 ......
The Epistle of Barnabas	.... 1360 ......
The Gospel according to the Hebrews	.... 2200 ......

This list gives us really valuable information as to the length of the book. We will put next to it a statement of similar character from a different source. The *Codex Claromontanus* D$_2$, of St Paul's Epistles, of the sixth century, has a catalogue in Latin of all the Scriptures, remarkable for many reasons, which Dr Zahn takes to be of Alexandrian origin (it is undoubtedly rendered from a Greek original) and of the third or fourth century in date. The concluding items in this are :

Epistle of Barnabas	850	verses (i.e. lines).
Revelation of John	1200	....
Acts of the Apostles	2600	....
The Shepherd	4000	....
Acts of Paul	3560	....
Revelation of Peter	270	....

A third list, which may be of A.D. 600, and is very commonly called the List of the Sixty Books, is less interesting. It gives us, among New Testament Apocrypha :

[1] Zahn, *N. T. Kanon*, ii. 290 sqq.

The History of James (i.e. the 'Protevangelium ').
The Apocalypse of Peter.
The Travels, and Teachings, of the Apostles.
The Epistle of Barnabas.
The Acts of Paul.
The Apocalypse of Paul.
&c.   &c.

Let us summarise the information we have gained from all these passages. The Apocalypse of Peter was a Greek book containing 270 or 300 lines of the average length of a line of Homer (36 to 38 letters) and about a quarter as long as the Revelation of S. John; or, in other words, about the length of the *Didache* as we have it (316 lines) or the Epistle to the Galatians (311 lines).

It probably found a partial reception at Rome in the second century; certainly it did in Egypt, and in Lycia; in Palestine it survived and was still read in church on Good Friday in the fifth century.

It continued to be copied down to the ninth century in Jerusalem (for the list of Nicephorus was made for practical purposes): and as we are told that the Gizeh MS. is of a date between the eighth and twelfth centuries, we may say the same of Egypt.

But all this while the popularity and reception of the book were not universal. If the Muratorian Fragment does mention it, it is with a caution : if Methodius quotes it, he does so without naming his source : while Eusebius and Sozomen are unqualified in their repudiation of it as a genuine work of the Apostle, and tell us that the use made of it by the great writers who had preceded them was practically *nil*. Macarius would not at all object to throwing it over: one of our lists calls it a *disputed* book, another places it among Apocrypha, and the third, whose author probably might have accepted it, gives it a place among writings which form a sort of appendix to the undoubted portion of the New Testament Canon.

So that, though no doubt it was a popular book, its popularity seems to have been almost confined to the less educated class of Christians. Clement is no doubt an exception to this statement: but few writers are less discriminating than he, though there are few who are better informed; while, if I read Methodius rightly, he is unwilling to lay much stress on the source which he uses, and uses sparingly.

I cannot attempt to give anything like a full account of what modern writers have written about this Apocalypse, albeit the bulk of matter is not very large. J. E. Grabe first collected the fragments in his *Spicilegium*, I. 74. Fabricius added some notes in *Cod. Apocr. N. T.*, I. 940. Lücke, in his *Introduction to the Revelation of S. John*, Lipsius, *Dict. Chr. Biogr.*, art. 'Apocalypses,' Hilgenfeld, *Nov. Test. extra Can. rec.*, IV. 74 (1866 and 1883), Dr Salmon in a lecture on *Uncanonical Books*, now embodied in his *Introduction to the New Testament*, Zahn, *N. T. Kanon*, II. 810—820, Robinson, *Passion of S. Perpetua*, pp. 37—43, should be consulted: they contain practically all that has as yet been said about the Apocalypse of Peter.

It is necessary before we pass to the second section of my paper to call special attention to two hypotheses: one, put forward by Bunsen in his *Analecta Ante-Nicaena*, is a suggestion that one source which was used by Hippolytus in his fragment 'Concerning the Universe' was the Apocalypse of Peter: the other, which is Mr Robinson's, is that we may find traces of this same Apocalypse in the *Passion of S. Perpetua*, and in *Barlaam and Josaphat*. I think the

new discovery goes some way towards confirming both conjectures.

We will now read the new fragment, which I have
divided into twenty short sections; and short notes will be
given on such points as suggest themselves. My rendering
will be literal and bald.

1. " ' Many of them will be false prophets, and will
teach ways and various doctrines of perdition: and they
will be sons of perdition. And then will God come unto
my faithful ones that are hungering and thirsting and
suffering oppression, and proving their own souls in this
life; and He will judge the sons of lawlessness.'

2. And the Lord said furthermore 'Let us go unto the
mountain and pray.' And as we twelve disciples went with
Him, we besought Him that He would shew us one of our
righteous brethren that had departed from the world, that
we might see of what form they were and so take courage
and encourage them also that should hear us.

3. And as we were praying, there suddenly appeared
two men standing before the Lord towards the *east, whom*[1]
we could not look upon: for there came from their countenance a ray as of the sun and *all* their raiment was light,
such as never eye of man *beheld, nor* mouth can describe,
nor heart *conceive* the glory wherewith they were clad, and
the beauty of their countenance.

And when we saw them we were amazed: for their
bodies were whiter than any snow, and redder than any
rose, and the red thereof was mingled with the white, and,
in a word, I cannot describe the beauty of them: for their
hair was thick and curling and bright, and beautiful upon
their face and their shoulders like a wreath woven of spike-

---

[1] Italics indicate words supplied where a gap occurs in the MS.

nard and bright flowers, or like a rainbow in the sky, such was their beauty.

4.   When, therefore, we saw their beauty, we were all amazement at them, for they had appeared suddenly : and I came near to the Lord and said : 'Who are these?' He saith to me : 'These are your brethren the righteous, whose forms ye wished to behold.' And I said to Him : 'And where are all the righteous, or of what sort is the world wherein they are and possess this glory?'

5.   And the Lord shewed me a very great space outside this world shining excessively with light, and the air that was there illuminated with the rays of the sun, and the earth itself blooming with unfading flowers, and full of spices and fair-flowering plants, incorruptible and bearing a blessed fruit : and so strong was the perfume that it was borne even to us from thence.   And the dwellers in that place were clad in the raiment of angels of light, and their raiment was like their land : and angels ran about (*or* encircled) them there.   And the glory of the dwellers there was equal, and with one voice they praised the Lord God, rejoicing in that place.   The Lord saith unto us : 'This is the place of your predecessors (*perh.* brethren) the righteous men.'

6.   And I saw also another place over against that other, very squalid, and it was a place of chastisement; and those that were being chastised, and the angels that were chastising, had their raiment dark, according to the atmosphere of the place.

7.   And there were some there hanging by their tongues ; and these were they that blaspheme the way of righteousness : and there was beneath them fire flaming and tormenting them.

8.   And there was a certain great lake full of flaming

mire, wherein were certain men that pervert righteousness; and tormenting angels were set upon them.

9. And there were also others, women, hung by their hair over that mire that bubbled up: and these were they that had adorned themselves for adultery: and the men that had been joined with them in the defilement of adultery *were hanging* by their feet, *and* had their heads in the mire: *and all* were saying 'We believed not that we should come into this place.'

10. And I saw the murderers and them that had conspired with them cast into a certain narrow place full of evil reptiles and being smitten by those beasts and wallowing there thus in that torment: and there were set upon them worms as it were clouds of darkness. And the souls of them that had been murdered were standing and looking upon the punishment of those murderers, and saying 'O God, righteous is thy judgment.'

11. And hard by that place I saw another narrow place wherein the gore and the filth of them that were tormented ran down, and became as it were a lake there. And there sat women having the gore up to their throats, and over against them a multitude of children *which* were born out of due time sat crying: and there proceeded from them *flames* (*or* sparks) of fire, and smote the women upon the eyes[1]. And these were they that *destroyed their children* and caused abortion.

12. And there were other *men* and women on fire up to their middle and cast into a dark place and scourged by evil spirits and having their entrails devoured by worms that rested not: and these were they that persecuted the righteous and delivered them up.

13. And hard by them again were women and men

[1] See Fragment 4.

gnawing their lips, and being tormented, and receiving red-hot iron upon their eyes : and these were they that had blasphemed and spoken evil of the way of righteousness.

14. And over against these were again other men and women gnawing their tongues and having flaming fire in their mouths: and these were the false witnesses.

15. And in a certain other place were pebbles sharper than swords or than any spit, red-hot, and women and men clad in filthy rags were rolling upon them in torment: and these were the wealthy that had trusted in their wealth and had not had pity upon orphans and widows, but had neglected the commandment of God.

16. And in another great lake full of pitch and blood and boiling mire stood men and women, up to their knees : and these were they that lent money and demanded interest on interest.

17. *And there were* other men and women being hurled down from a great cliff, and they reached the bottom and again were driven by those that were set upon them to climb up upon the cliff, and thence they were hurled down again, and they had no rest from this torment.

[These were guilty of lewdness.]

18. And beside that cliff was a place full of much fire, and there stood men who had made for themselves images instead of God with their own hands.

19. And beside them were other men and women who had rods, smiting each other, and never resting from this manner of torment.

20. And others again near them, women and men were burning, and turning themselves and being roasted: and these were they that had forsaken the way of God."

Here we have a fragment of sufficient length to give us a fair idea of the contents of the whole Apocalypse. As a fact, it does contain something like 140 out of the original 300 lines of which the book consisted.

It falls into three parts: the first is the eschatological discourse, § 1: the second, the vision of Paradise, §§ 2—6: the third, the Inferno, §§ 7—20.

We will take them separately. The first gives the concluding lines of a speech of our Lord concerning the end of the world.

The opening clause recalls, and is doubtless indebted to, Matt. xxiv. 24; Mark xiii. 22, 'For there shall arise false Christs and *false prophets.*' But both this and the words which follow contain the first of a remarkable series of resemblances to the Second Epistle of Peter, which I propose to collect in a note, in order that we may be the better able to realise them[1].

[1] *Apoc.* § 1. πολλοί...ἔσονται ψευδοπροφῆται.

2 Pet. ii. 1 ἐγένοντο δὲ καὶ ψευδοπροφῆται ἐν τῷ λαῷ, ὡς καὶ ἐν ὑμῖν ἔσονται, ψευδοδιδάσκαλοι, and iii. 3.

καὶ...δόγματα...τῆς ἀπωλείας διδάξουσιν.

2 Pet. ii. 1 οἵτινες παρεισάξουσιν αἱρέσεις ἀπωλείας.

δοκιμάζοντας τὰς ἑαυτῶν ψυχάς. 2 Pet. ii. 8 ψυχὴν δικαίαν... ἐβασάνιζεν.

ὁ θεὸς...κρινεῖ τοὺς υἱοὺς τῆς ἀνομίας.

2 Pet. ii. 3 οἷς τὸ κρίμα ἔκπαλαι οὐκ ἀργεῖ.

§ 2. τὸ ὄρος.

2 Pet. i. 18 σὺν αὐτῷ ὄντες ἐν τῷ ἁγίῳ ὄρει.

τῶν ἐξελθόντων ἀπὸ τοῦ κόσμου.

2 Pet. i. 15 μετὰ τὴν ἐμὴν ἔξοδον.

ποταποί εἰσι τὴν μορφήν.

2 Pet. iii. 11 ποταποὺς δεῖ ὑπάρχειν ὑμᾶς.

§ 7. τόπον...αὐχμηρόν.

2 Pet. i. 19 ἐν αὐχμηρῷ τόπῳ.

§ 7 (and § 13). οἱ βλασφημοῦντες τὴν ὁδὸν τῆς δικαιοσύνης.

2 Pet. ii. 2 δι᾽ οὓς ἡ ὁδὸς τῆς ἀληθείας βλασφημηθήσεται.

ibid. 21 ἐπεγνωκέναι τὴν ὁδὸν τῆς δικαιοσύνης.

What the bearing of these resemblances may be upon the vexed question of the authenticity of 2 Peter, I will not take it upon myself to determine: only, it must be remembered that three explanations of them are possible. Either the author of the Apocalypse designedly copied the Epistle (as S. Jude may also have done), or the Apocalypse and Epistle are products of one and the same school, or the resemblances do not exist.

We will return to the consideration of the text.

Have we any parallel to the fragment of the discourse put into our Lord's mouth? No doubt it is ultimately modelled on the discourse in Matt. xxiv.; Mark xiii.; Luke xxi. But there is an Apocryphal document which helps us here very considerably. It is a book which exists in Syriac, Carshunic, and Ethiopic. It has been published in Syriac by Lagarde, who has also made a retranslation into

κολαζόμενοι.

2 Pet. ii. 9 οἶδεν Κύριος...ἀδίκους...εἰς ἡμέραν κρίσεως κολαζομένους τηρεῖν.

§ 8. βόρβορος. § 15. ἐκυλίοντο.

2 Pet. ii. 22 εἰς κυλισμὸν βορβόρου.

§§ 9, 11, 17. Punishment of impurity.

2 Pet. ii. 10 sqq. Denunciations of impurity.

§ 15. ἀμελήσαντες τῆς ἐντολῆς τοῦ θεοῦ.

2 Pet. ii. 21 ὑποστρέψαι ἐκ τῆς...ἁγίας ἐντολῆς.

iii. 2 ἐντολῆς τοῦ κυρίου.

To these, the following resemblances in the smaller fragments must be added.

Fragments 1, 2.

The heaven and earth are to be judged.

2 Pet. iii. 10 οὐρανοὶ ῥοιζηδὸν παρελεύσονται.

12 οὐρανοὶ πυρούμενοι λυθήσονται.

Fragment 6.

ἐκ τῶν ἁμαρτιῶν γεννᾶσθαι (τὰς κολάσεις) φησίν.

2 Pet. ii. 19 ᾧ γάρ τις ἥττηται, τούτῳ δεδούλωται.

Greek, the original language[1]. Its proper name is 'The first book of Clement, which is called the Testament of our Lord Jesus Christ: the words which He spake to His holy Apostles after He had risen from the dead.'

Now, I am of the opinion that this book, or at least the first fourteen chapters of it, gives us a very fair idea of the lost first part of the Apocalypse of Peter. It is expanded by various rhetorical additions, from prophecy and gospel, but the resemblances are constant, and, I think, striking. Let us examine them.

In the first place, the general complexion of both books is the same. Both contain a speech of our Lord dealing with the last things: only, that in the Testament is more complete.

Secondly, the situation seems to be the same in both: namely, that our Lord is addressing the disciples *after* the Resurrection. In the Testament, He is questioned by Peter and John, in presence of the other Apostles. In the Apocalypse, Peter is the questioner; the other Apostles are present. But it is not made absolutely clear at what point in our Lord's career the vision is being revealed. The portion of the book which would have told us is gone: yet one touch makes it likely that the time meant is,—in the Apocalypse as in the Testament,—the time after the Resurrection. For the Apostles ask to see the glory of Paradise, in order that they may thereby be enabled to encourage their hearers[2]. This implies that at that moment they had already received their commission to preach. (Such a commission, be it noted, is given in the opening section of the Testament.) The words of Christ 'Let us

[1] Syriac in *Reliquiae Juris Eccl. Antiquiss. Syriace:* Greek in *Rel. Jur. Eccl. Ant. Graece.* 1856.
[2] § 2.

go to the mount and pray' (§ 2), point in the same direction. The date imagined by our author can hardly be that of Matt. xxiv., for there the discourse was delivered *on* the Mount of Olives: here the transition to the Mount takes place *after* the discourse is over.

Thirdly, there are coincidences of language:

Apocalypse.	*Testament.*
1. Many of them will be false prophets, and will teach ways and various doctrines of perdition : and they will be sons of perdition.	8. There shall rise up shepherds who shall be lawless, etc. etc., men of much talk [1], opposing the ways of the Gospel, dishonouring all the way of piety: they shall appoint commandments to men not according to the scripture and the commandment which the Father would have.
	3, etc. The expression 'son of perdition' is used of Antichrist.
	10. 'Sons of destruction' used of the Phoenicians, in the sense of 'doomed.'
And then shall God come unto my faithful ones that hunger and thirst, and are oppressed, and prove their souls in this life.	8. They shall be upright, pure, contrite...many shall be oppressed and shall call on their God that they may be saved.
	They shall teach them that if they prove their spirit [2] they will be fit for the kingdom.
	14. I therefore have told you this, that wherever ye go ye may prove the holy souls [3].

In both documents the actual coming of God is described in the most unemphatic way.

[1] πολύλαλοι, Lagarde.

[2] ἐὰν δοκιμάσωσι τὸ πνεῦμα αὐτῶν, Lag.

[3] δοκιμάσητε τὰς ψυχὰς τὰς ὁσίας, Lag.

Apocalypse.	*Testament.*
1. God shall come.	12. The harvest is come, that the guilty may be reaped and the Judge appear suddenly and confront them with their works.

Both discourses end at the same point. After the discourse in the Apocalypse, the Lord says 'Come to the mount;' and then the vision is seen. In the Testament, after the mention of the judgment, He says, 'Turn therefore unto the churches, and administer them'; and the rest of the book is occupied with legislation.

I think that considering that the merest shred of the discourse survives in the Apocalypse, these coincidences are remarkable. But there is more evidence to come. I shall ask you to examine with me the Second Book of the Sibylline Oracles, a book which is assigned either to the 3rd or early 4th century[1].

Of this book, ll. 6—30, 154—213, contain a description of the signs of the end, of which one source is evidently, I think, a document resembling the Testament.

Sib. Orac.	*Testament.*
21 — 38. General slaughter, plagues, famine, destruction of unjust rulers.	3, 4, 5. Plagues, famine, unjust rulers, slaughter: a wicked king in the West: slaughter:
Sudden peace and plenty.	'Silver shall be despised and gold honoured.' Also cf. 8 *sub fin.*
A great star in heaven like a crown[2].	6. Signs in heaven: a bow, a horn, and a torch.
[39—154. Poem of Pseudo-Phocylides with introduction and epilogue.]	7. Signs on earth: monstrous births: children whose 'appear-

[1] I shall make use of the excellent edition of Rzach, 1891.

[2] The star is modified into a crown, as it seems, in order to introduce the poem attributed to Phocylides (56—148): this poem is a collection of moral precepts, and the star represents the crown given to the keeper of the law of God.

Sib. Orac.	*Testament.*
155. Children born grey-headed (cf. Hesiod, *Op.* 181).	ance shall be as of those advanced in years: for they that are born shall be white-haired.'
General affliction.	8. Evil shepherds.
False prophets.	General confusion and wicked-
Beliar (Antichrist).	ness: the remnant remain faithful.
Return of the lost tribes.	9, 10. The son of perdition
The faithful servants keep watch.	described.
Elias comes.	

The Sibylline book goes on to describe the destruction of the world by fire, the resurrection, and the judgment: and in this second half has many points of connexion with our *Apocalypse:* as the *Testament* does not treat of these matters we can follow it no further just now.

Only, let the point which I am trying to enforce be borne in mind: the Testament may represent the lost first part of the Apocalypse: the Sibyl does use the second part, as I hope to shew: also, the Sibyl in *her* first part resembles the Testament. Is it not *a priori* likely that she uses the Apocalypse all through?

Two more points in connexion with the Testament, and I have done: first it comes to us in a Petrine form, for it is attributed to Clement the companion of Peter. (And there exists in Arabic and Ethiopic an Apocalypse of Peter of which Clement is the ostensible redactor[1].) So that it is linked by this fact with the spurious Petrine literature: and additionally by the fact that the two Apostles who are specially named as speakers are Peter and John.

Secondly, though there is as yet no trace of the spread of the Testament in the West, I have recently come upon

---

[1] This book is being examined and analysed for me: I hope to produce parts of it at a later time. It is my hope that the old Apocalypse will be found imbedded in it.

a fragment in Latin, containing the exact equivalent of §§ 11 and 7 (in that order), namely, the description of Antichrist, and the signs upon earth. This exists in an Uncial MS. of the 8th century, and, though I possibly ought to include it in this essay, I propose to print it in a forthcoming number of *Texts and Studies*. My own belief is that it is a fragment of the Apocalypse of Peter: and that belief I base mainly on analogies in late Apocalypses which seem plainly dependent upon that book, and upon the great unlikeliness that the Testament was ever known in the West.

Returning to the text of the Apocalypse, we find that §§ 2—5 are occupied with a short vision of Paradise and of its inhabitants: and here, if anywhere, our author attains to a certain standard of literary excellence, although it does not seem as if Paradise were his favourite subject of contemplation.

Our illustrative parallels are less numerous here: the most striking one is a vision in which Mr Robinson[1] conjectured that some trace of the influence of the Apocalypse was discoverable, — namely, the vision of Josaphat in the *History of Barlaam and Josaphat*[2]. I will translate the passages, and call attention (in the notes) to such coincidences of language as exist.

Josaphat "saw himself caught away by certain terrible beings, and passing through places which he had never seen, and arriving at a plain of vast extent[3], flourishing with fair and very sweet-smelling flowers[4], where he saw

---

[1] *Passion of S. Perpetua*, p. 37.

[2] Boissonade, *Anecd. Graeca* iv. pp. 280, 360.

[3] μεγίστην πεδιάδα: cf. μέγιστον χῶρον *Apoc.* § 5.

[4] ὡραίοις ἄνθεσι καὶ λίαν εὐώδεσι κομώσῃ: cf. γῆν...ἀνθοῦσαν ἀμαράντοις ἄνθεσι καὶ ἀρωμάτων πλήρη *ibid.*

plants of all manner of kinds, loaded with strange and wondrous fruits, most pleasant to the eye and desirable to touch[1]. And the leaves of the trees made clear music to a soft breeze and sent forth a delicate fragrance, whereof none could tire, as they stirred[2]....And through this wondrous and vast plain these fearful beings led him, and brought him to a city which gleamed with an unspeakable brightness and had its walls of translucent gold, and its battlements of stones the like of which none has ever seen....And a light from above ever darted its rays and filled all the streets thereof: and certain winged hosts, each to itself a light[3], abode there singing in melodies never heard by mortal ears; and he heard a voice saying: This is the rest of the righteous: this is the joy of them that have pleased the Lord[4]."

Again in a later part of the book[5], the vision is continued, thus:

" He saw those fearful men, whom he had seen before, coming to him, and taking him away to that vast and wondrous plain, and bringing him into the glorified and exceeding bright city[6]. And as he was entering into the gate, others met him, all radiant with light, having crowns

[1] φυτὰ παντοδαπὰ καὶ ποικίλα, καρποῖς ξένοις...καὶ θαυμαστοῖς βρίθοντα : cf. φυτῶν εὐανθῶν καὶ ἀφθάρτων καὶ καρπὸν εὐλογημένον φέροντα ibid.

[2] cf. τοσοῦτον δὲ ἦν τὸ ἄνθος ὡς καὶ ἐφ' ἡμᾶς ἐκεῖθεν φέρεσθαι ibid.

[3] Cf. οἱ δὲ οἰκήτορες...ἐνδεδυμένοι ἦσαν ἔνδυμα ἀγγέλων φωτινῶν... ἄγγελοι δὲ περιέτρεχον αὐτοὺς ἐκεῖσε...καὶ μιᾷ φωνῇ τὸν κύριον θεὸν ἀνευφήμουν, εὐφραινόμενοι (εὐφροσύνη is the word for 'joy' in the Vision of Josaphat) ibid.

[4] cf. οὗτός ἐστιν ὁ τόπος τῶν ἀδελφῶν (?) ὑμῶν τῶν δικαίων ἀνθρώπων ibid.

[5] p. 360.

[6] ὑπέρλαμπρον : cf. ὑπέρλαμπρον τῷ φωτί ibid.

in their hands which shone with unspeakable beauty[1], and such as mortal eyes never beheld[2]: and when Josaphat asked: 'Whose are the exceeding bright[3] crowns of glory which I see?' 'One' they said 'is thine'."

I think the obligation is really unmistakable here. But it may perhaps be remembered, that, in the place where he quotes this vision, Mr Robinson establishes a connexion between it and the Vision of Saturus. Does that vision help us here? I will quote some lines from it which seem clearly to do so. 'And when we had passed *the first world*, we saw an infinite light.' How does this compare with the words 'the Lord shewed me a vast space *outside this world*'? (§ 5). Again: 'and whilst we were being borne along by those four angels, there was made for us (we came upon) *a great space*, which was like a garden, *having rose-trees and flowers of all sorts*. The height of the trees was after the manner of a cypress, and the leaves of them sang without ceasing.' The flowers and plants of § 5 will be remembered in this connexion.

After they had passed over the 'violet-grown stadium' and come to the city built of light, four angels 'clothed us as we entered in with white garments' (§ 5 the dwellers had the garb of angels of light, § 3 all their raiment shone). 'We heard *an united voice* saying Holy, Holy, Holy without ceasing' (§ 5 all *with one voice* were praising the Lord God): again 'we began there to recognise many *brethren*' (cf. § 2).

Lastly, at the end of the vision, it is said, 'we were nourished by *an unspeakable perfume*, which satisfied us,'

---

[1] cf. οὐ δύναμαι ἐξηγήσασθαι τὸ κάλλος αὐτῶν § 3.

[2] οἵους ὀφθαλμοὶ οὐδέποτε βρότειοι ἐθεάσαντο: cf. ὁποῖον οὐδέποτε ὀφθαλμὸς ἀνθρώπ[ων ἑώρακεν or ἐθεάσατο] § 3.

[3] ὑπέρλαμπροι: see above.

(§ 5 'so great was the perfume that it was borne even to us from thence').

Surely, with these proofs before us, we may safely affirm that the Martyrs of Africa had read the Apocalypse of Peter, and that Mr Robinson's hypothesis is confirmed by the new discovery.

We must pass to the consideration of the Inferno.

First, I will examine the contribution of the Vision of Josaphat to the elucidation of this part. After he has seen the beautiful city, he is removed[1], much against his will, to the infernal regions. 'And when they had passed through that great plain, they brought him to certain places, dark, and full of all foulness[2], whose horror counterbalanced the brightness which he had seen. Here was a furnace kindled and aflame with fire[3]; and a sort of worm, fashioned for punishment, crept about there[4]. And chastising powers[5] stood over the furnace, and there were certain men being miserably burned in the fire. And a voice was heard saying 'This is the place of sinners[6]: this is the punishment[6] of them that have defiled themselves with shameful deeds[7].' And thereupon, they led him forth.'

The resemblances here are not so striking, perhaps, as in the vision of Paradise, but they are real resemblances, notwithstanding.

We will take next the evidence of the Second Book of the Sibylline Oracles. The poet has described the destruc-

---

[1] l.c. p. 281.

[2] cf. αὐχμηρὸν πάνυ...σκοτινόν, κατὰ τὸν ἀέρα τοῦ τόπου *Apoc.* 6.

[3] cf. πῦρ φλεγόμενον καὶ κολάζον αὐτούς 7, and *passim.*

[4] cf. πεπληρωμένον ἑρπετῶν πονηρῶν ... σκώληκες ὥσπερ νεφέλαι σκότους 10: and ὑπὸ σκωλήκων ἀκοιμήτων 12.

[5] cf. οἱ κολάζοντες ἄγγελοι 7 : ἐπέκειντο αὐτοῖς ἄγγελοι βασανισταί 9.

[6] cf. καὶ ἦν τόπος κολάσεως 7.

[7] cf. §§ 10, 17.

tion of heaven and earth, the resurrection, and the judgment: all, it is then said, will pass through a fiery stream :
the good will be saved, but the bad will perish for 'whole
aeons': and then the classes of sinners are enumerated[1].

'Those *who did murder, or who were privy to it*[2], liars,
deceitful thieves, violent house-plunderers, gluttons, un-
faithful in wedlock, those who pour forth *wicked words*[3],
the terrible ones, the violent, the lawless, *the idolaters*[4] and
those who have *forsaken* the great immortal *God*[5], and
become *blasphemers* and harmers of the pious[6], and breakers
of faith and *destroyers of just men*[7]: deceitful priests and
deacons who judge unjustly...worse than leopards and
wolves, the proud, 'and *usurers who collect interest on
interest*[8] in their houses and *injure orphans and widows*[9] in
every way': fraudulent or grudging almsgivers, those who
forsake their aged parents, or disobey or curse their parents,
deniers of a trust committed to them, servants who turn
against their masters, those *who defile their flesh*[10], unchaste
maidens, *causers of abortion*[11], and *those who expose their
children*[12], and sorcerers, male and female.

These all shall be brought to the pillar round which runs
the fiery stream: 'and them all shall the undying *angels* of
the immortal and eternal God, having bound them fast with
unbreakable chains, *chastise*[13] most terribly with scourges of
flame and chains of fire: and then shall cast them into the

[1] l. 255 sqq.
[2] cf. § 10 murderers, and those who were their accomplices : συνίστορες
Sib. = συνειδότας *Apoc.*
[3] cf. §§ 7, 13.   [4] cf. § 18.
[5] cf. § 20.   [6] cf. § 13.
[7] cf. § 12.   [8] cf. § 16.
[9] cf. § 15.   [10] cf. §§ 9, 17.
[11] cf. § 11.   [12] cf. Fragments 3, 5.
[13] Cf. the tormenting angels in §§ 6, 8, 17.

gloom of night[1] in Gehenna among the *beasts of Hell*[2], many
and terrible, where the *darkness*[1] is infinite': then follows
the fiery wheel and river: they suffer triple torment for each
sin, but eventually a hope of salvation, by means of the
prayers of the good, is held out (ll. 330—335).

The resemblances, or, as I hold them to be, the traces
of obligation to our Apocalypse in the Sibylline book, are
fully made out, I venture to think, in the case of the classes
of sinners: they are not so striking, though they exist, in
the description of torment. But it is clear that in a poem
which is dealing in prediction and not describing things
seen, details of this kind would be out of place.

Let us pass next to a vision contained in the early 3rd
century novel (if it be not of the 2nd century) the Acts of
Thomas[3]. In this, a woman whom S. Thomas has raised from
the dead, narrates what she has seen in the infernal regions.
Here again the borrowings from our Apocalypse are so considerable, that I must translate nearly the whole passage.
The woman says: 'A certain man took me, who was hateful
to look upon, entirely black, and his raiment very foul[4]:
and he brought me to a place wherein were many chasms,
and much stench[5] and a horrible exhalation proceeded from
thence. And he made me look into every chasm: and in
the (first) chasm I saw *flaming fire*, and wheels of fire were
turning there[6], and souls hung upon those wheels, and were
dashed against each other: and there was a great crying
and howling there, but there was none to help. And that
man said to me: 'These souls are of thy race, and for a set

---

[1] cf. § 6.   [2] cf. §§ 10, 12.

[3] *Acta Thomae*, ed. Bonnet, p. 39.

[4] The dark raiment of the tormentors § 6. The ῥάκη ῥυπαρά § 18.

[5] δυσωδία: so § 11.

[6] ἔτρεχον ἐκεῖσε: cf. ἄγγελοι περιέτρεχον αὐτοὺς ἐκεῖσε § 5.

number of days they have been delivered over into torment and breaking, and then others are brought in in their stead, and they likewise are transferred to another place: these are they that have *perverted the union* of man and woman[1]. And I looked and saw *infants* heaped upon one another and struggling with one another, and lying on each other[2]. And he answered and said to me: These are their children, and therefore they are set here as a testimony against them.

'He brought me to another chasm, and I looked in and saw *mire*[3] and *the worm*[4] *bubbling up*[5] and souls wallowing there, and a great gnashing of teeth was heard from them, and that man said to me: These are the souls of women that have forsaken their husbands and committed adultery with other men, and have been brought into this torment[6].

'He shewed me another chasm whereinto I looked, and saw souls, some *hanging by their tongue*[7], some by their *hair*[8], some by their hands, some by their *feet, head downwards*[9], and being smoked with fire and brimstone; concerning whom that man that was with me answered me: These souls that are hung by their tongue are slanderers, and uttered false and shameful words; and those that hang by their hair, it is further explained, were bold-faced people who went about bare-headed in the world: those hung by their hands were cheats and never gave to the poor: those hung by their feet ran after pleasure, but did not visit the sick nor bury the dead.'

The woman then sees the cave where souls are imprisoned

[1] cf. §§ 9, 17.   [2] cf. § 11.
[3] §§ 8, 9, 16.   [4] §§ 10, 12.
[5] ἀναβρύοντα: cf. ἀναπαφλάζοντος § 9, ἀναζέοντος § 16.
[6] cf. § 9.   [7] cf. § 7.
[8] cf. § 9.   [9] cf. § 9.

before torment, and, after a short colloquy between her guide and the other chastising spirits, is taken back to the world.

I hope my readers will take the trouble to compare for themselves my translation of this vision with the references to the Apocalypse which I have printed. To my mind, they are conclusive in favour of an obligation to the Apocalypse of Peter.

The next witness to be examined is the Apocalypse of Paul; which I may be forced to call simply '*Paul*' for shortness' sake. This book we have in a rather shortened text of the original Greek, in a fuller Syriac version, and in a Latin version which is the fullest of all. This last is in print, and I hope it will be published shortly in a forthcoming number of *Texts and Studies*. It is of course advisable to quote the Greek where we have it; but it will probably be necessary to refer to the Latin too. The abbreviations G and L will serve to show which is meant.

Paul is, as I have elsewhere remarked[1], a book of the fourth or early fifth century, and a mosaic made out of more than one earlier book: and it has already been noticed (by Hilgenfeld and Salmon) that the use of the name 'Temeluchus' as the name of an angel is a mark that the writer had seen the Apocalypse of Peter. For this word occurs in Fragments 3 and 5; it is really an adjective, and means 'caretaking': but it is quite peculiar to this book, and might well have been misunderstood by a later writer. But this mistake of *Paul* does not seem to have been followed up by those who have called attention to it. Had this been done, it would have been clear that Paul had borrowed much more than one word from our Apocalypse; and this we shall see when we come to examine

---

[1] *Texts and Studies* ii. 2. 21.

the Fragments. At present we are to look for resemblances
to the *text* of the Apocalypse.

Paul G 19 'the place of the just[1].' *Apoc. Pet.* 5 'the place
                of your brethren (?) the just men.'

  ,,   ,,   22 'trees planted, full of different fruits.' *Pet.* 5.

  ,,   ,,   23 'the light (of the city) was beyond the light of the
                world.' *Pet.* 5 'exceeding bright with light[2].'

  ,,   ,,   27 'when he passes out of the world.' *Pet.* 5 'out-
                side this world[3].'

  ,,   ,,   17, 18 'great is thy judgment.' *Pet.* 10.

  ,,   ,,   18 the souls of the murdered are introduced. cf.
                Pet. 10.

  ,,   ,,   31 'there was no light there, but darkness.' *Pet.* 6.

  ,,   ,,   16 'a multitude of men and women *cast* therein.'
                Pet. 10 'murderers...*cast* in a certain place[4].'

  ,,   ,,   31 'some up to their knees.' *Pet.* 16 'up to their
                knees.'

  ,,   ,,   32 'but trusted in the vanity of their wealth.' *Pet.*
                15 'that trusted in their wealth.'

  ,,   ,,   35 'the widow and orphan he did not pity.' *Pet.*
                15 'that pitied not orphans and widows.'

  ,,   ,,   37 'eating their tongues.' *Pet.* 14 'gnawing their
                tongues.'

  ,,   ,,   39 'being led away into a dark place. *Pet.* 12
                'cast into a dark place[5].'

  ,,   ,,   40 'standing upon fiery spits.' *Pet.* 15 'sharper
                than any spit heated[6].'

[1] τὸν τόπον τῶν δικαίων.

[2] φῶς...ὑπὲρ τὸ φῶς τοῦ κόσμου: cf. ὑπέρλαμπρον τῷ φωτί.

[3] ἐξερχόμενος ἐκ τοῦ κόσμου: cf. ἐκτὸς τοῦ κόσμου τούτου.

[4] βεβλημένους ἐν αὐτῷ: cf. βεβλημένους ἔν τινι τόπῳ, and § 12.

[5] ἀπαγομένας ἐν τόπῳ σκοτινῷ: cf. βεβλημένοι ἐν τόπῳ σκοτινῷ.

[6] ἐπάνω ὀβελίσκων πυρίνων: cf. ὀξύτεροι...παντὸς ὀβελίσκου πεπυρωμένοι.

Paul G 40 'these are they that corrupted themselves and killed their children[1].' *Pet.* 11 'these were they that destroyed and made abortive their children.'

„ *L* 37 and 39 'and worms devouring them.' *Pet.* 10 and 12.

„ „ 'these are they that demanded interest on interest and trusted in their riches.' *Pet.* 10 and 15[2].

„ „ 38 'into this pit flow all the punishments.' *Pet.* 11[3].

„ „ 40 'and beasts tearing them.' *Pet.* 10 'being smitten by these beasts.'

„ „ 41 'there was straitness, and the mouth of the well was strait.' *Pet.* 10, 11 'a strait place[4].'

„ „ 42 'the worm that is restless'. *Pet.* 12[5].

„ „ 39 'girls in black raiment,' 40 'men and women clothed in rags full of pitch and sulphur.' *Pet.* 15 'men and women clothed in foul rags,' and 6 'raiment like the atmosphere of the place.'

Some little time back I called attention to a conjecture of Bunsen's that in the fragment *Concerning the Universe* Hippolytus might have made use of our Apocalypse. In his *Missing Fragment of the Fourth Book of Ezra*, Professor

---

[1] αὗται εἰσιν αἱ φθείρασαι ἑαυτὰς καὶ τὰ βρέφη αὐτῶν ἀποκτείνασαι. The text of *Peter* here is partly conjectural.

[2] Hii sunt qui usuras usurarum exigentes et confidentes in diuiciis suis. Cf. οὗτοι .. οἱ .. ἀπαιτοῦντες τόκους τόκων (16) and τῷ πλούτῳ αὐτῶν πεποιθότες (15).

[3] In istam foueam influunt omnes pene: cf. ἐν ᾧ ὁ ἰχὼρ τῶν κολαζομένων κατέρρεε.

[4] angustia, et angustum erat: cf. ἐν τόπῳ τεθλιμμένῳ.

[5] uermem inquietum: cf. σκωλήκων ἀκοιμήτων.

Bensly has shown that one of Hippolytus' sources is
4 Esdras. But I think it is fairly clear that the Apocalypse
of Peter was another.

'Hades[1] is a place in the creation which is unfurnished[2],
a locality underground wherein the light of the world does
not shine,' so far there is nothing Petrine. 'Now since no
light shines[3] in this place, darkness must constantly prevail
there. This place is appointed as a prison for souls, and
over it are appointed angel-warders, who administer the
temporary chastisements of the places in accordance with
the deeds of each soul[4].'

'There is one way down to the place, and at the gate,
as we have learned to believe, there stands an archangel
with his host...the just are escorted in light to the right...
and led to a shining place wherein dwell the righteous that
were from the beginning.' And there they enjoy the expectation of complete joy. 'But the wicked are dragged to
the left by chastising angels, not going any longer willingly,
but being haled by force as captives, and the angels deride
and reproach them and thrust them downwards' to a place
where they dwell in sight of Paradise and of Gehenna, but
with a great gulf between them and the righteous. Peter's
Inferno, it will be remembered, was 'over against Paradise'
(§ 6), and was full of chastising angels (§§ 6, 8). At the last
judgment all men and angels and demons will join in saying
'Just is thy judgment[5].' Emphasis is laid on the 'worm of
fire, not dying nor destroying the body, but continually pro-

---

[1] *S. Hippolyti Opera*, ed. Lagarde, p. 68.

[2] τόπος ἀκατασκεύαστος from Enoch xxi. 1, 2 (Gizeh fragment).

[3] φωτὸς μὴ καταλάμποντος: cf. *Pet.* 5.

[4] ἄγγελοι φρουροί, πρὸς τὰς ἑκάστων πράξεις διανέμοντες τὰς τῶν τόπων
κολάσεις: cf. *Pet.* 6, 8.

[5] μίαν φωνὴν ἀποφθέγξονται...Δικαία σου ἡ κρίσις: cf. *Pet.* 5, 10.

ceeding from the body with ceaseless pain.' And in general
it may be said that though *Peter* is not the only source
employed, he is most likely one source.

There are yet two other Apocalypses of a considerably
later date than *Paul*, which bear almost as clear traces of
the influence of the Apocalypse of Peter: these are the
Apocalypse of Esdras[1] and that of the Virgin. The former
contains an *Inferno* scattered in various parts of the book,
if so confused a patch-work as this document is can be dig-
nified with the name of a book. The torments and sins
described show one remarkable coincidence with the
Apocalypse[2]. The latter[3] is one long dreary *Inferno* of the
weakest kind, but shows a large number of coincidences.
It may be worth while to cite some passages when we come
to discuss the Fragments: but I will ask my readers to trust
for the present my assertion of the obligations of these two
documents to our Apocalypse: the evidence which I could
adduce is not different in kind from that of which I have
already given a good deal.

One additional proof of the influence of the description
of Paradise may here be given. It comes from a book
variously called the Narrative or Apocalypse of Zosimas[4], a
hermit who went to visit the Blessed Ones, the descendants
of the Rechabites, in their earthly Paradise. He was carried
over the river which separates the heavenly land from ours
by two trees which bent down and wafted him over: these
trees were 'fair and most comely, full of sweet-smelling fruit[5].'

---

[1] Tischendorf, *Apocall. Apocr.* 24—33.

[2] See below, on the Fragments.

[3] Not yet printed, so far as I know: it is very common in MSS., and
I have transcribed it for publication.

[4] To be published in *Texts and Studies* with other like documents.

[5] γέμοντα καρπὸν εὐωδίας.

When he arrived in the land he found it to be a place 'full of much fragrance ; and there was no mountain on one side or the other, but that place was a plain full of flowers, all begarlanded, and all the land was fair[1].'

The first man whom he met wore no garments, and when Zosimas asked the reason of this, he bade him look up into the sky and behold his raiment: 'and I looked and saw his face as the face of an angel and his garment as the lightning which shineth from east to west, and I feared that he was the Son of God[2].' Compare this with the description of Paradise and its inhabitants in *Pet.* 3, 5. It should be recorded here that the author of *Zosimas* elsewhere borrows a sentence from the *Protevangelium;* which shows his proclivities.

In the Ethiopic 'Conflict of Matthew[3],' the dwelling-place of the lost 9½ tribes is described (in a passage which practically recurs in Commodian's poems[4]): and it is said that 'when the wind blows, we smell through it the smell of gardens. In our land there is neither summer nor winter, neither cold nor hoar-frost, but on the contrary a breath of life[5].'

We must now turn to the discussion of the Fragments. Fragments 1 and 2 are those furnished by Macarius Magnes,

---

[1] ἦν ὁ τόπος ἐκεῖνος πλήρης εὐωδίας πολλῆς, καὶ οὐκ ἦν ὄρος ἔνθα καὶ ἔνθα, ἀλλ' ἦν ὁ τόπος ἐκεῖνος πεδινὸς ἀνθοφόρος, ὅλος ἐστεφανωμένος, καὶ πᾶσα ἡ γῆ εὐπρεπής.

[2] θεάσαι τὸ ἔνδυμά μου ποῖόν ἐστιν. καὶ θεασάμενος ἐν τῷ οὐρανῷ εἶδον τὸ πρόσωπον αὐτοῦ ὡσεὶ πρόσωπον ἀγγέλου (Act. vi. 15) καὶ τὸ ἔνδυμα αὐτοῦ ὡς ἀστραπήν, ἡ ἐξ ἀνατολῶν εἰς δυσμὰς πορευομένη.

[3] Malan, *Conflicts of the Holy Apostles*, p. 44.

[4] *Instr.* ii. 1, *Carm. Apol.* 940 sqq.

[5] I believe it to be the case that the author of the *Carmen de Iudicio Domini* used our book; and Commodian may have done so as well; but in his case the number of sources used is considerable.

or rather, by the heathen writer whom he undertakes to confute. I will translate and comment on them in order.

"Let us by way of superfluity cite also that saying in the Apocalypse of Peter. It introduces the heaven as being about to undergo judgment along with the earth, in these terms. 'The earth,' it says, 'shall present all men before God at the day of judgment, being itself also to be judged along with the heaven also which encompasses it'." And he goes on to inquire why the heaven is to be destroyed seeing that it is the Creator's noblest work. Then, in the following chapter, we find: "This, moreover, it says, which is a saying full of impiety: 'And every power of heaven shall be melted, and the heaven shall be rolled up like a scroll, and all the stars shall fall like leaves from a vine, and as leaves fall from a fig tree'." With this we should compare Isa. xxxiv. 4, where the words are identical, save that the 'powers of heaven' are in the plural; and in view of this fact, the passage has been looked upon by some (e.g. Hilgenfeld) as merely a quotation from Isaiah, and not from the Apocalypse. Yet the way in which the heathen objector brings it forward, the way in which Macarius answers it, the fact that we find it partially quoted in our Lord's eschatological discourse (Luke xxi. 26) and in the Apocalypse of John (vi. 13, 14), are considerations which, when combined, lead me to think that Zahn does right when he includes it among the fragments.

In this prophecy of the destruction of heaven and earth, we have, as Dr Salmon has pointed out, a trait which is prominent in another Petrine work, the Second Epistle, which, alone among New Testament books, predicts the destruction of the world by fire. And, further, we have a gap at the beginning of our Apocalypse to which a prophecy of this sort would be the best possible supplement. It must have found a place in the prophetic speech of our Lord, of which we have the scanty remains in § 1.

Moreover, a book which, we have seen reason to believe, has used our Apocalypse, devotes some space to a description of the destruction of the world by fire, namely, the Second Book of the Sibylline Oracles[1]. Again, S. Methodius, who quotes the Apocalypse, lays stress on this point too[2]. The third century poet Commodian has a line which seems an echo of the prophecy that the heaven is to be judged: 'the stars of heaven fall, the stars are judged with us[3],' and certainly Commodian used several apocryphal sources.

Fragments 3—6 all bear on one and the same subject, and may be translated together.

3. "The scripture says that the infants that have been exposed (i.e. cast out in the street at their birth) are delivered to a caretaking angel, by whom they are educated, and so grow up; and they will be, it says, as the faithful of an hundred years old are here."

Then, in what I take to be a separate extract, though hitherto it has been printed continuously with the last[4], there follows :

4. "Wherefore also Peter in the Apocalypse says: 'And a flash of fire darting from those children, and smiting the eyes of the women '."

Here we have, in slightly different language, an extract

---

[1] ll. 190—213.

[2] *De Resurr.* ap. Epiph. *Haer.* lxiv. 31.

[3] *Carm. Apol.* 1004.

[4] My reasons for making the division are these: (1) the unique MS. does not itself divide the extracts. (2) §§ 39, 40 are plainly divided wrongly by the editors. (3) The particle Διό has no sense, if connected with the preceding sentence. As an extract detached from the context, the fragment is intelligible: § 48 begins with αὐτίκα.

from our text (§ 11). It is the only one which is identifiable as such among the fragments.

5 *a*. "For instance, Peter in the Apocalypse says that the children who are born untimely shall be of the better part: and that these are delivered over to a caretaking angel that they may attain a share of knowledge and gain the better abode, after suffering what they would have suffered if they had been in the body: but the others shall merely obtain salvation as injured beings to whom mercy is shewn: and remain without punishment, receiving this as a reward."

5 *b*. "Whence also we have received in divinely inspired Scriptures that untimely births are delivered to caretaking angels, even if they be the offspring of adultery. For, had they come into existence contrary to the will and ordinance of that blessed nature of God, how could they have been delivered to angels to be brought up in great quietness and refreshment? and how could they with boldness have summoned their own parents to the Judgment-seat of Christ, to accuse them? saying: 'Thou, O Lord, didst not grudge us that light which is common to all: but these exposed us to death, despising Thy commandment'."

6. "'But the milk of the women, flowing from their breasts and congealing,' says Peter in the Apocalypse, 'shall engender small beasts (*perhaps* serpents) that consume flesh: and these run up upon them and devour them': teaching us that the punishment comes on account of the sin (i.e. is suited to the nature of the sin). He says that they (the punishments) are born of the sins, just as for its sins the people was sold, and because of their unbelief towards Christ, as the Apostle says, they were bitten by serpents (1 Cor. x. 9)."

In Fragments 3 and 5 we have some puzzling problems.

Let us, if possible, set out quite clearly the assertions which are made.

1. Exposed infants are given to an angel, and educated, and attain a condition like that of an aged Christian.

(Fr. 3.)

2. Untimely births are given to an angel, and go through the experience of life.

Another class is merely not punished.   (Fr. 5 a.)

3. A certain class of children (probably untimely births) is given to angels, even if born of adultery; and is educated in a place of peace: they accuse their parents of exposing them to death.

And for these facts the Apocalypse of Peter, the 'Scripture', and 'divinely-inspired writings' are given as authorities.

Our text of the Apocalypse tells us about the punishment of the causes of untimely births, but it says nothing of infants exposed to death after birth.

First, can we find reason for supposing that all the fragments which I have quoted here came from the Apocalypse? Zahn denies that they do: he attributes Fr. 3 and Fr. 5 b to some unknown book[1]: principally on the ground that, reading § xli. of Clement as one paragraph, we have the same book quoted twice, once without a name, once under its proper name: which is impossible: therefore two books are quoted.

But I have already shewn sufficient reason for dividing the paragraph into two, as I think; and with this division, the difficulty to a large extent disappears.   Clement, in two adjacent passages of a continuous text (in which he

---

[1] He also reads παραδίδοται for παραδίδοσθαι in 5 a, so as to confine the Petrine quotation to the first sentence of the paragraph: but this is really quite arbitrary.

was very probably commenting on the Book of Wisdom) has twice quoted our Apocalypse, introducing his quotations in slightly different terms. I think there is no other reason for denying the Petrine origin of the passage.

Let me give my own theory of the reconstruction of the Fragments. They belong to the lost part of the *Inferno*, and to the explanations of things seen which must there have been given to Peter either by our Lord or by an angel. Peter has seen the women and the children born untimely (as in § 11): later on he sees women who have exposed their children, instead of suckling them: the milk of these unnatural mothers, which ought to have been given to their children, has engendered small serpents, which devour their flesh (Fr. 6).

After the vision is over, Peter asks for explanation of certain parts of it. He is told, in particular, of the destinies of the two classes of children, untimely births, and exposed children. The untimely births are given over to a care-taking angel, and attain experience, and mature condition (Fr. 3, 5 *a b*). They accuse their parents at the bar of Christ (Fr. 5 *b*). The exposed children only gain salvation in the shape of immunity from punishment (Fr. 5 *a*), presumably because they have been actually born, and have consequently entered the ranks of human life.

Now to comment on the fragments, and see what can be drawn from them in justification of this reconstruction.

Fr. 3 speaks of the *exposed* infants being given over to the angel, and, in fact, treated in the way elsewhere predicated of the untimely births. I am forced to regard the word *exposed*[1] as an inaccuracy of Clement's, or else as a wrong reading for *abortive*, which latter word can be obtained by a slight change. But the theory that it is an

---

[1] ἐκτεθέντα: what is wanted is ἐκτρωθέντα.

inaccuracy is preferable; because the whole quotation is made in the most general terms possible: we have the same passage accurately (or more accurately) reproduced by Clement himself in Fr. 5 a and by Methodius in 5 b.

Very likely Clement is here commenting on a passage of Ecclesiastes (vi. 3, 4) where a long life and an untimely birth are compared together[1]. The words of Isaiah 'the child shall die an hundred years old[2]' may be also in his mind. Notice that the word *faithful* occurs in § 1 of our text. The clause in which this word occurs corresponds to the clause in 5 a, which is a paraphrase by Clement, 'in order that they may attain a share of knowledge, etc.'

4. The difference of language between this fragment and our text might lead one to suspect that the latter is a shortened one, or that Clement is quoting from memory. If the word '*flash*' be original it can be paralleled from *Paul G* 35[3]. Clement goes on to quote a text from Wisdom (iii. 7, 8) comparing the righteous to a spark among the stubble.

5 a, b. The unique word for '*caretaking*[4]' is made into a proper name in *Paul* and in the later 'Apocalypse of John[5],' and is applied to a chastising angel[6]. But, in effect, *Paul* has done much more than borrow a single word: in *G* 40 we have the following passage, which at once takes us back to the source of Fr. 5 b.

"And the angel said to me 'These are they that defile themselves, and that killed their children. The children

[1] ἐὰν γεννήσῃ ἀνὴρ ἑκατόν, καὶ ἔτη πολλὰ ζήσεται...ἀγαθὸν ὑπὲρ αὐτὸν τὸ ἔκτρωμα.

[2] Isa. lxv. 7.

[3] ἐφλέγετο δεινῶς ὑπὸ ἀστραπῶν.   [4] τημελοῦχος.

[5] Tischendorf, *Apocall. Apocr.* 70—94: see p. 94.

[6] §§ 16, 34.

therefore came crying: 'Avenge us of our parents.' And
they were given to an angel, that they should be taken to a
place of ease, but their parents to eternal fire." In *L* 40,
the text is fuller (the Syriac omits the whole section).

"And he answered me: 'These are women that defiled
the image of God, (untimely) bringing forth infants from the
womb, and these are the men that caused the sin. But
their children appeal unto the Lord God and the angels
which are over the punishments, saying: 'Avenge us of our
parents: for they have defiled the image of God, having the
name of God, but not keeping his commandments: they
gave us to be devoured of dogs and trampled upon by swine,
and others they cast into the river.' But those children
were given to the angels of Tartarus which were over the
punishments, that they should take them to a place of ease
and mercy. But their fathers and mothers were taken to
eternal punishment[1]."

Paul does not make it quite clear whether he is speaking
of infants born untimely or exposed after birth: his words
would apply to both classes. But this is of little moment,
for we are not dealing with a quotation, but with a plagiarism,

---

[1] Et respondit mihi: Haec sunt mulieres commaculantes ($\phi\theta\epsilon i\rho\alpha\sigma\alpha\iota$)
plasmam dei proferentes ($\dot{\epsilon}\kappa\rho\dot{\omega}\sigma\alpha\sigma\alpha\iota$) ex utero infantes, et ii sunt uiri
concubentes cum eis. Infantes autem earum interpellant dominum
deum et angelos qui super penas erant, dicentes: Nefanda ora (*sic*. I
read: Vindica nos a) genitoribus nostris: ipsi enim commaculauerunt
plasma dei, nomen dei abentes, sed praecepta eius non obseruantes
dederunt nos in escam canibus et in conculcationem porcis: alios
proiecerunt in flumine. Infantes autem illi traditi sunt angelis tartari
qui erant super penas (the Latin invariably changes Temeluchus to
Tartaruchus), ut ducerent in locum spaciosum misericordiae. Patres
autem et matres eorum strangulabantur in perpetuam poenam. 'Stran-
gulabantur' seems to be a rendering of $\dot{\alpha}\pi\dot{\eta}\gamma\chi\theta\eta\sigma\alpha\nu$, which is a mis-
reading for $\dot{\alpha}\pi\dot{\eta}\chi\theta\eta\sigma\alpha\nu$, the word indicated in the Greek.

and a certain amount of intentional variation is to be expected. An authority, cited earlier as having made use of our book, mentions both classes; this is the Sibyl[1].

The two offences are specially forbidden in the *Didache*, and in Barnabas' Epistle. And no doubt it would be possible to collect a good deal of somewhat unsavoury evidence to show the common occurrence of them in the ancient world. The writer of the *Letter to Diognetus* makes especial mention of the freedom of Christians from this form of guilt. 'They marry and beget children, like all the world: but they do not cast out the children when born.' And the Apostolical Constitutions (vii. 3), in amplifying the prohibition of these sins in the *Didache*, add words which recall those of *Paul* and of Clement (Fr. 5 *a*) 'For everything that is fashioned in the likeness of man, and has received a soul from God, if it be murdered shall be avenged, having been unjustly slain[2].'

I may note that, in the tract which Hilgenfeld calls the 'Judgment of Peter' and others the 'Ecclesiastical Canons,' the prohibition of these sins is put into the mouth of Peter,

---

[1] *Sib. Or.* ii. 280.   ὅσσαι δ' ἐνὶ γαστέρι φόρτους
ἐκτρώσκουσιν, ὅσοι τοκετοὺς ῥίπτουσιν ἀθέσμως.

And in the Pseudo-Phocylides, part of which is interpolated in the same book, we have the same two sins mentioned, in a way which recalls the Latin *Paul*, viz. l. 184.

μηδὲ γυνὴ φθείροι βρέφος ἔμβρυον ἔνδοθι γαστρός,
μηδὲ τεκοῦσα κυσὶν ῥίψῃ καὶ γυψὶν ἕλωρα.

Cf. 'in escam canibus, etc.' of *Paul*.

[2] φονευθὲν ἐκδικηθήσεται, ἀδίκως ἀναιρεθέν. It should be remarked, lastly, that the use of so strange a word as τημελοῦχος suits well with the habit of our author. Other uncommon words used by him are ναρδόσταχυς, ὑπέρλαμπρος, οἰκήτωρ, ἀνευφημεῖν, ἀναπαφλάζειν, ἰχώρ, χάλιξ, τηγανίζω.

which, whether the author intended a reference to the Apocalypse or not, is a very appropriate attribution.

Fr. 6. This belongs to a description of torment seen by Peter in a part of the *Inferno* which either followed our text, or has dropped out of it. It almost certainly refers to the punishment of those mothers who *exposed* their children. Compare the following fragment from the Apocalypse of Esdras (p. 29) "And I saw a woman hanging, and four beasts[1] (*or* serpents) sucking her breasts. And the angels said to me: 'This woman grudged to give her milk, and also cast her children into rivers.'"

This quotation throws a good deal of light on our fragment. We see at once that the meaning of it is that the milk of those women who exposed their children became the means of their punishment. They refused it to their children, and it engendered the serpents which devoured them. And the principle here inculcated, that the nature of the sin determines the nature of the punishment, is one which runs through a large part of our Apocalypse, and through almost all the later visions. It is an important one, specially prominent in Dante's *Inferno*, and I believe that it originated with the Apocalypse of Peter.

Fr. 7. I have added this to the list, without any misgivings, for it appears to me to contain a distinct reminiscence of §§ 7 and 9 of our Apocalypse[2].

Hilgenfeld includes among the fragments a quotation twice made by Hippolytus from 'the prophet,' and found also in Commodian's *Carmen Apologeticum* (886—90). If it is really from our Apocalypse, which, judging from the

---

[1] θηρία. The Apocalypse of the Virgin contains two or three very similar descriptions.

[2] Cf. especially βλασφημιῶν, and τὰς διὰ κόσμου τριχῶν ἐπὶ πορνείαν ὁρμώσας.

terms in which it is introduced, I am rather inclined to
doubt, it must have formed part of the introductory section
in which the end of the world was predicted.   It runs thus:
"And another prophet also says: 'He (Antichrist) shall
gather all his forces from the East even unto the West:
those whom he hath summoned and those whom he hath
not summoned[1] shall go with him: he shall whiten[2] the sea
with the sails of his ships and blacken[3] the plain with the
shields of his weapons: and every one that shall encounter
him in battle shall fall by the sword' (*Of Antichrist*, c. 15
and 54).

During all this discussion, I have taken it for granted
that the fragment before us is part of the Apocalypse of
Peter; yet the seer's name is nowhere given.   Is it certain
that it is not meant for the work of someone else?   The
reasons which lead me to suppose that it does belong to the
Apocalypse of Peter are as follows:

(1)   It is attributed to one of 'us the twelve disciples'
(an expression which, by the way, occurs in the Gospel also,
and is inaccurate in both places) § 2.

(2)   The author is the spokesman of the twelve disciples
§ 4.

(3)   A passage occurs in it which is substantially identical with a quotation from the Apocalypse of Peter.

(4)   We know of no other Apocalypse attributed to an
Apostle which it would be possible to identify with this
fragment, save, perhaps, the Revelation of Thomas: and it
is really very doubtful whether that book ever existed.

It is probable that the lost end of the book contained

---

[1] οὓς κεκλήκοι καὶ οὓς οὐ κεκλήκοι.   [2] λευκανεῖ.

[3] μελανεῖ. The vocabulary is curious, and, so far, is an argument
for the Petrine origin.   The use of κεκλήκοι is so odd that one is tempted
to guess that it is a rendering of a Latin 'uocauerit.'

the substance of Fr. 6, some explanations of the vision given by our Lord to Peter, and less certainly, some account of what happens to souls immediately after death.

I have thus brought to an end a long and perhaps desultory investigation of this very interesting fragment. Many questions of high importance I have designedly left on one side[1]: many more I have, no doubt, failed through ignorance to ask. But I have tried to put into the hands of students the main results of a somewhat laborious examination of Christian Apocalyptic literature. And I hope that, however unattractive may be the subjects treated by Pseudo-Peter and by myself, and whatever the defects of their treatment, I have made it clear to students both of theology and of literature that they have in this book a document of the highest importance. How many of our popular notions of heaven and hell are ultimately derived from the Apocalypse of Peter, I should be sorry to have to determine. But I think it is more than possible that a good many of them are; and that when we sing in church of a land where

> everlasting spring abides,
> And never-withering flowers,

we are very likely using language which could be traced back with few gaps, if any, to an Apocalypse of the second century.

---

[1] The relation of the classes of sinners named in the Apocalypse to those found in the *Didache*; the connexion of the *Ritual of the Dead*, the *Pistis Sophia*, and the *Apocalypse of Zephaniah* with our book, are among these, as also the questions whether we have reason to suppose that our text of the Apocalypse is a shortened one, and whether the author of the Apocalypse did not write the ' Gospel ' as well.

I append a short note on resemblances between the *Didache* and our Apocalypse.

Didache.	Apoc.
2. οὐ φονεύσεις	10
οὐ μοιχεύσεις	9
οὐ παιδοφθορήσεις...	17
οὐ φονεύσεις τέκνον ἐν φθορᾷ, οὐδὲ γεννηθὲν ἀποκτενεῖς...	11
οὐ ψευδομαρτυρήσεις...	14
οὐκ ἔσῃ πλεονέκτης	16
3. ὀργή	? 19
φόνος	10
μοιχεῖαι	9
εἰδωλολατρεία	18
φιλάργυρος	16
βλασφημία	7, 13
5. φόνοι	10
μοιχεῖαι, ἐπιθυμίαι, πορνεῖαι...	9
εἰδωλολατρεῖαι...	18
ψευδομαρτυρίαι...	14
διῶκται ἀγαθῶν...	12
οὐκ ἐλεοῦντες πτωχόν	15
φονεῖς τέκνων, φθορεῖς πλάσματος θεοῦ (cf. *Paul, Lat.* 40)	11
ἀποστρεφόμενοι τὸν ἐνδεόμενον, καταπονοῦντες τὸν θλιβόμενον	15
πλουσίων παράκλητοι	15

The *Pistis Sophia* has a certain number of coincidences in vocabulary (especially in pp. 117—243 of the Latin translation): the words αἰών, ἄρχοντες (possibly in Apoc. 5 we should read ἀρχόντων for ἀρχέρων), τόπος, μορφή, κόσμος, κόλασις, are all prominent. In pp. 237—243 a series of sins and their punishments is described: the sins are, abusive language, slander, murder, theft, pride, blasphemy, impurity. The punishments do not correspond with those in our book. However, the general situation is the same; revelations are imparted by the Lord to the disciples after the Resurrection. I have little doubt that the Apocalypse is, like the *Pistis Sophia*, of Egyptian origin, and that both have connexions with the *Ritual of the Dead.*

ΕΥΑΓΓΕΛΙΟΝ ΚΑΤΑ ΠΕΤΡΟΝ.

1 ...τ[ῶν] δὲ Ἰουδαίων οὐδεὶς ἐνίψατο τὰς χεῖρας, Mt xxviii 24
οὐδὲ Ἡρώδης οὐδ᾽ εἷς τῶν κριτῶν αὐτοῦ. καὶ βουληθέντων
νίψασθαι ἀνέστη Πειλᾶτος. καὶ τότε κελεύει Ἡρώδης ὁ Lc xxiii 11
βασιλεὺς παρ[αλημ]φθῆναι τὸν Κύριον, εἰπὼν αὐτοῖς ὅτι
5 Ὅσα ἐκέλευσα ὑμῖν ποιῆσαι αὐτῷ, ποιήσατε.

2. Ἥκει δὲ ἐκεῖ Ἰωσὴφ ὁ φίλος Πειλάτου καὶ τοῦ
Κυρίου, καὶ εἰδὼς ὅτι σταυρίσκειν αὐτὸν μέλλουσιν ἦλθεν
πρὸς τὸν Πειλᾶτον καὶ ᾔτησε τὸ σῶμα τοῦ Κυρίου πρὸς
ταφήν. καὶ ὁ Πειλᾶτος πέμψας πρὸς Ἡρώδην ᾔτησεν Lc xxiii 7
10 αὐτοῦ τὸ σῶμα· καὶ ὁ Ἡρώδης ἔφη Ἀδελφὲ Πειλᾶτε, εἰ
καὶ μή τις αὐτὸν ᾐτήκει, ἡμεῖς αὐτὸν ἐθάπτομεν, ἐπεὶ καὶ
σάββατον ἐπιφώσκει. γέγραπται γὰρ ἐν τῷ νόμῳ ἥλιον Lc xxiii 54
μὴ δῦναι ἐπὶ πεφονευμένῳ πρὸ μιᾶς τῶν ἀζύμων τῆς [Eph iv 26];
cf. Jn xix 31
ἑορτῆς αὐτῶν.

15 3 Οἱ δὲ λαβόντες τὸν Κύριον ὤθουν αὐτὸν τρέ-
χοντες καὶ ἔλεγον Σύρωμεν τὸν υἱὸν τοῦ θεοῦ, ἐξουσίαν Jn xix 10 f.
αὐτοῦ ἐσχηκότες· καὶ πορφύραν αὐτὸν περιέβαλλον, καὶ Mc xv 17
ἐκάθισαν αὐτὸν ἐπὶ καθέδραν κρίσεως λέγοντες Δικαίως Jn xix 13
κρῖνε, βασιλεῦ τοῦ Ἰσραήλ. καί τις αὐτῶν ἐνεγκὼν
20 στέφανον ἀκάνθινον ἔθηκεν ἐπὶ τῆς κεφαλῆς τοῦ Κυρίου. ‖
καὶ ἕτεροι ἑστῶτες ἐνέπτυον αὐτοῦ ταῖς ὄψεσι, καὶ ἄλλοι τὰς Mt xxvi 67 f.

2 οὐδ᾽ εἷς] οὐδεὶς   καὶ] καὶ [τῶν]   3 νίψασθαι.
Ἀνέστη Πειλάτης καὶ   5 ἐκέλευ(η)σα   16 εὔρωμεν·
forsitan legendum εὔρομεν uel ἄρωμεν

6—2

Jn xix 34 σιαγόνας αὐτοῦ ἐράπισαν· ἕτεροι καλάμῳ ἔνυσσον αὐτόν·
καί τινες αὐτὸν ἐμάστιζον λέγοντες Ταύτῃ τῇ τιμῇ τιμή-
σωμεν τὸν υἱὸν τοῦ θεοῦ.

4 Καὶ ἤνεγκον δύο κακούργους καὶ ἐσταύρωσαν ἀνὰ
μέσον αὐτῶν τὸν Κύριον. αὐτὸς δὲ ἐσιώπα ὡς μηδένα 5
πόνον ἔχων. καὶ ὅτε ὥρθωσαν τὸν σταῦρον ἐπέγραψαν
ὅτι Οὗτός ἐστιν ὁ βασιλεὺς τοῦ Ἰσραήλ. καὶ τεθεικότες
τὰ ἐνδύματα ἔμπροσθεν αὐτοῦ διεμερίσαντο καὶ λαχμὸν

Lc xxiii 39 ff. ἔβαλον ἐπ᾽ αὐτοῖς. εἷς δέ τις τῶν κακούργων ἐκείνων
ὠνείδισεν αὐτοὺς λέγων Ἡμεῖς διὰ τὰ κακὰ ἃ ἐποιήσαμεν 10
οὕτω πεπόνθαμεν· οὗτος δὲ σωτὴρ γενόμενος τῶν ἀνθρώπων. τί ἠδίκησεν ὑμᾶς; καὶ ἀγανακτήσαντες ἐπ᾽ αὐτῷ

Jn xix 32 ἐκέλευσαν ἵνα μὴ σκελοκοπηθῇ, ὅπως βασανιζόμενος ἀπο-
θάνοι.

5 Ἦν δὲ μεσημβρία, καὶ σκότος κατέσχε πᾶσαν τὴν 15
Ἰουδαίαν· καὶ ἐθορυβοῦντο καὶ ἠγωνίων μήποτε ὁ ἥλιος
ἔδυ, ἐπειδὴ ἔτι ἔζη· γέγραπται [γὰρ] αὐτοῖς ἥλιον μὴ
δῦναι ἐπὶ πεφονευμένῳ. καί τις αὐτῶν || εἶπεν Ποτίσατε

Jn xix 28, 29 (vv.ll.) αὐτὸν χολὴν μετὰ ὄξους· καὶ κεράσαντες ἐπότισαν, καὶ
ἐπλήρωσαν πάντα, καὶ ἐτελείωσαν κατὰ τῆς κεφαλῆς 20
αὐτῶν τὰ ἁμαρτήματα. περιήρχοντο δὲ πολλοὶ μετὰ

Jn xviii 3, 6 λύχνων νομίζοντες ὅτι νύξ ἐστιν, ἔπεσάν τε. καὶ ὁ
Κύριος ἀνεβόησε λέγων Ἡ δύναμίς μου, ἡ δύναμις,
κατέλειψάς με. καὶ εἰπὼν ἀνελήφθη. καὶ αὐτῆς ὥρας
διεράγη τὸ καταπέτασμα τοῦ ναοῦ τῆς Ἰερουσαλὴμ εἰς 25
δύο.

Jn xx 25 6 Καὶ τότε ἀπέσπασαν τοὺς ἥλους ἀπὸ τῶν χειρῶν
τοῦ Κυρίου, καὶ ἔθηκαν αὐτὸν ἐπὶ τῆς γῆς· καὶ ἡ γῆ πᾶσα

2 τιμήσαμεν, fors. leg. ἐτιμήσαμεν uel τιμήσομεν
5 ἐσιώπα ὡς μηδένα] ἐσιωπάσας μηδὲν   6 ὅτι ἐώρθωσαν
10 ὠνείδησεν   15 μεσεμβρία   16 ἐθορουβοῦντο   ἠγώνισαν
17 ἔδυε fors. leg. ἔδυσε   17 om. γὰρ   18 πεφονευμένῳ
21 περιέρχοντο   22 ἔπεσάν τε] ἐπέσαντο   24 αὐτῆς] αὐτὸς

ἐσείσθη, καὶ φόβος μέγας ἐγένετο. τότε ἥλιος ἔλαμψε Mt xxvii 51
καὶ εὑρέθη ὥρα ἐνάτη· ἐχάρησαν δὲ οἱ Ἰουδαῖοι, καὶ δεδώ-
κασι τῷ Ἰωσὴφ τὸ σῶμα αὐτοῦ ἵνα αὐτὸ θάψῃ, ἐπειδὴ
θεασάμενος ἦν ὅσα ἀγαθὰ ἐποίησεν. λαβὼν δὲ τὸν
5 Κύριον ἔλουσε καὶ εἴλησε σινδόνι καὶ εἰσήγαγεν εἰς Mc xv 46
ἴδιον τάφον, καλούμενον κῆπον Ἰωσήφ.   Jn xix 41

7 Τότε οἱ Ἰουδαῖοι καὶ οἱ πρεσβύτεροι καὶ οἱ ἱερεῖς,
ἰδόντες οἷον ‖ κακὸν ἑαυτοῖς ἐποίησαν, ἤρξαντο κόπτεσθαι
καὶ λέγειν Οὐαὶ ταῖς ἁμαρτίαις ἡμῶν· ἤγγισεν ἡ κρίσις Lc xxiii 48
10 καὶ τὸ τέλος Ἰερουσαλήμ. ἐγὼ δὲ μετὰ τῶν ἑταίρων   (v.l.)
μου ἐλυπούμην, καὶ τετρωμένοι κατὰ διάνοιαν ἐκρυβό-
μεθα· ἐζητούμεθα γὰρ ὑπ' αὐτῶν ὡς κακοῦργοι, καὶ ὡς
τὸν ναὸν θέλοντες ἐμπρῆσαι. ἐπὶ δὲ τούτοις πᾶσιν ἐνη-
στεύομεν καὶ ἐκαθεζόμεθα πενθοῦντες καὶ κλαίοντες νυκτὸς
15 καὶ ἡμέρας ἕως τοῦ σαββάτου.   cf. Jn xx 26

8 Συναχθέντες δὲ οἱ γραμματεῖς καὶ Φαρισαῖοι καὶ Mt xxvii
πρεσβύτεροι πρὸς ἀλλήλους, ἀκούσαντες ὅτι ὁ λαὸς   62 ff.
ἅπας γογγύζει καὶ κόπτεται τὰ στήθη λέγοντες ὅτι Εἰ Lc xxiii 48
τῷ θανάτῳ αὐτοῦ ταῦτα τὰ μέγιστα σημεῖα γέγονεν, ἴδετε
20 ὅτι πόσον δίκαιός ἐστιν· ἐφοβήθησαν οἱ πρεσβύτεροι, καὶ
ἦλθον πρὸς Πειλᾶτον δεόμενοι αὐτοῦ καὶ λέγοντες Παρά-
δος ἡμῖν στρατιώτας, ἵνα φυλάξωσι τὸ μνῆμα αὐτοῦ ἐπὶ
τρεῖς ἡμ[έρας], μήποτε ἐλθόντες ‖ οἱ μαθηταὶ αὐτοῦ
κλέψωσιν αὐτόν, καὶ ὑπολάβῃ ὁ λαὸς ὅτι ἐκ νεκρῶν
25 ἀνέστη καὶ ποιήσωσιν ἡμῖν κακά. ὁ δὲ Πειλᾶτος
παραδέδωκεν αὐτοῖς Πετρώνιον τὸν κεντυρίωνα μετὰ
στρατιωτῶν φυλάσσειν τὸν τάφον· καὶ σὺν αὐτοῖς ἦλθον
πρεσβύτεροι καὶ γραμματεῖς ἐπὶ τὸ μνῆμα, καὶ κυλίσαντες
λίθον μέγαν μετὰ τοῦ κεντυρίωνος καὶ τῶν στρατιωτῶν
30 ὁμοῦ πάντες οἱ ὄντες ἐκεῖ ἔθηκαν ἐπὶ τῇ θύρᾳ τοῦ μνή-

1 ἐγείσθη	2 εὑρήθη	5 σινδόνι[ν]
13 ἐνηστένομεν	16 εὐναχθέντες	22 φυλάξω
27 στρατιωτόν	29 μετὰ] κατὰ	30 ὁμοὶ

ματος· καὶ ἐπέχρισαν ἑπτὰ σφραγῖδας, καὶ σκηνὴν ἐκεῖ
πήξαντες ἐφύλαξαν.

9 Πρωΐας δὲ ἐπιφώσκοντος τοῦ σαββάτου ἦλθεν
ὄχλος ἀπὸ Ἰερουσαλὴμ καὶ τῆς περιχώρου, ἵνα ἴδωσι τὸ
μνημεῖον ἐσφραγισμένον· τῇ δὲ νυκτὶ ᾗ ἐπέφωσκεν ἡ 5
κυριακή, φυλασσόντων τῶν στρατιωτῶν ἀνὰ δύο δύο κατὰ
φρουράν, μεγάλη φωνὴ ἐγένετο ἐν τῷ οὐρανῷ, καὶ εἶδον
ἀνοιχθέντας τοὺς οὐρανοὺς καὶ δύο ἄνδρας ‖ κατελθόντας
ἐκεῖθε, πολὺ φέγγος ἔχοντας, καὶ ἐπίσταντας τῷ τάφῳ·
ὁ δὲ λίθος ἐκεῖνος ὁ βεβλημένος ἐπὶ τῇ θύρᾳ ἀφ’ ἑαυτοῦ 10
κυλισθεὶς ἐπεχώρησε παρὰ μέρος· καὶ ὁ τάφος ἠνοίγη, καὶ
ἀμφότεροι οἱ νεανίσκοι εἰσῆλθον.

10 Ἰδόντες οὖν οἱ στρατιῶται ἐκεῖνοι ἐξύπνισαν τὸν
κεντυρίωνα καὶ τοὺς πρεσβυτέρους· παρῆσαν γὰρ καὶ
αὐτοὶ φυλάσσοντες. καὶ ἐξηγουμένων αὐτῶν ἃ εἶδον, 15
πάλιν ὁρῶσιν ἐξελθόντας ἀπὸ τοῦ τάφου τρεῖς ἄνδρας, ‖
καὶ τοὺς δύο τὸν ἕνα ὑπορθοῦντας, καὶ σταυρὸν ἀκολου-
θοῦντα αὐτοῖς· καὶ τῶν μὲν δύο τὴν κεφαλὴν χωροῦ-
σαν μέχρι τοῦ οὐρανοῦ, τοῦ δὲ χειραγωγουμένου ὑπ’
αὐτῶν ὑπερβαίνουσαν τοὺς οὐρανούς· καὶ φωνῆς ἤκουον 20
ἐκ τῶν οὐρανῶν λεγούσης Ἐκήρυξας τοῖς κοιμωμένοις;
καὶ ὑπακοὴ ἠκούετο ἀπὸ τοῦ σταυροῦ ὅτι Ναί.

11 Συνεσκέπτοντο οὖν ἀλλήλοις ἐκεῖνοι ἀπελθεῖν ‖
καὶ ἐνφανίσαι ταῦτα τῷ Πειλάτῳ. καὶ ἔτι διανοουμένων
αὐτῶν φαίνονται πάλιν ἀνοιχθέντες οἱ οὐρανοί, καὶ ἄν- 25
θρωπός τις κατελθὼν καὶ εἰσελθὼν εἰς τὸ μνῆμα. ταῦτα

Mt xxviii 1

[1 Pe iii 19]

1 ἐπέχρεισαν   8 ἀνοιχθέντες   9 ἐπίσαντας
10 λεῖθος   11 fors. leg. ὑπεχώρησε   ἐνοίγη
15 αὐτοὶ] ἂν οἱ   16 ὅρασιν ἐξελθόντος   ἄνδρες
17 ἀκολοθοῦντα   19 τοῦ δὲ χειραγωγουμένου] τὸν δὲ
χεῖρα τῷ τουμένου   20 φωνῇ   21, 22 κοινωμένοις
καὶ ὑπακοῇ. ἠκούετο   22 ὅτι Ναί] τιναι
26 κατελθὸν

ἰδόντες οἱ περὶ τὸν κεντυρίωνα νυκτὸς ἔσπευσαν πρὸς
Πειλᾶτον, ἀφέντες τὸν τάφον ὃν ἐφύλασσον· καὶ ἐξηγή-
σαντο πάντα ἅπερ εἶδον, ἀγωνιῶντες μεγάλως καὶ λέγοντες
Ἀληθῶς υἱὸς ἦν θεοῦ. ἀποκριθεὶς ὁ Πειλᾶτος ἔφη Ἐγὼ
5 καθαρεύω τοῦ αἵματος τοῦ υἱοῦ τοῦ θεοῦ· ὑμῖν δὲ τοῦτο   Mt xxvii 24
ἔδοξεν. εἶτα προσελθόντες πάντες ἐδέοντο αὐτοῦ καὶ παρε-
κάλουν κελεῦσαι τῷ κεντυρίωνι καὶ τοῖς στρατιώταις μηδὲν
εἰπεῖν ἃ εἶδον. Συμφέρει γάρ, φασίν, ἡμῖν ὀφλῆσαι μεγίστην ἁμαρτίαν ἔμπροσθεν τοῦ θεοῦ, καὶ μὴ ἐμπεσεῖν εἰς
10 χεῖρας τοῦ λαοῦ τῶν Ἰουδαίων καὶ λιθασθῆναι. ἐκέλευ-
σεν οὖν ὁ Πειλᾶτος τῷ κεντυρίων[ι] καὶ τοῖς στρατιώταις
μηδὲν εἰπεῖν.

12 Ὄρθρου δὲ τῆς κυριακῆς Μαριὰμ ἡ Μαγδαληνή,
μαθήτρια τοῦ Κυρίου ([ἥτις] φοβουμένη διὰ τοὺς Ἰουδαίους,   cf. Jn xix 3
15 ἐπειδὴ ἐφλέγοντο ‖ ὑπὸ τῆς ὀργῆς, οὐκ ἐποίησεν ἐπὶ τῷ
μνήματι τοῦ Κυρίου ἃ εἰώθεσαν ποιεῖν αἱ γυναῖκες ἐπὶ   Jn xix 40
τοῖς ἀποθνήσκουσι καὶ τοῖς ἀγαπωμένοις αὐταῖς) λαβοῦσα
μεθ᾽ ἑαυτῆς τὰς φίλας ἦλθε ἐπὶ τὸ μνημεῖον ὅπου ἦν
τεθείς. καὶ ἐφοβοῦντο μὴ ἴδωσιν αὐτὰς οἱ Ἰουδαῖοι,
20 καὶ ἔλεγον Εἰ καὶ μὴ ἐν ἐκείνῃ τῇ ἡμέρᾳ ᾗ ἐσταυρώθη
ἐδυνήθημεν κλαῦσαι καὶ κόψασθαι, καὶ νῦν ἐπὶ τοῦ μνή·
ματος αὐτοῦ ποιήσωμεν ταῦτα. τίς δὲ ἀποκυλίσει ἡμῖν   Mc xvi 3 ff.
καὶ τὸν λίθον τὸν τεθέντα ἐπὶ τῆς θύρας τοῦ μνημείου,
ἵνα εἰσελθοῦσαι παρακαθεσθῶμεν αὐτῷ καὶ ποιήσωμεν
25 τὰ ὀφειλόμενα; μέγας γὰρ ἦν ὁ λίθος, καὶ φοβούμεθα
μή τις ἡμᾶς ἴδῃ. καὶ εἰ μὴ δυνάμεθα, κἂν ἐπὶ τῆς θύρας
βάλωμεν. ἃ φέρομεν εἰς μνημοσύνην αὐτοῦ, κλαύσομεν καὶ
κοψόμεθα ἕως ἔλθωμεν εἰς τὸν οἶκον ἡμῶν.

13 Καὶ ἀπελθοῦσαι εὗρον τὸν τάφον ἠνεῳγμένον·   Lc xxiv 2
30 καὶ προσελθοῦσαι παρέκυψαν ἐκεῖ, καὶ ὁρῶσιν ἐκεῖ τινὰ   Jn xx 5

3 ἀπανιῶντες   5 ἡμῖν   6 καίπερ ἐκάλουν
13 ὀρθοῦ   Μαγδαλινὴ   14 om. ἥτις   17 αὐτοῖς
21 κόψεσθαι   27, 28 fors. leg. κλαύσωμεν καὶ κοψώμεθα

Mc xvi 5 f. νεανίσκον καθεζόμενον μέσῳ τοῦ τάφου, ὡραῖον καὶ περι-
βεβλημένον || στολὴν λαμπροτάτην· ὅστις ἔφη αὐταῖς Τί
ἤλθατε; τίνα ζητεῖτε; μὴ τὸν σταυρωθέντα ἐκεῖνον; ἀνέστη
καὶ ἀπῆλθεν· εἰ δὲ μὴ πιστεύετε, παρακύψατε καὶ ἴδετε
τὸν τόπον ἔνθα ἔκειτο, ὅτι οὐκ ἔστιν· ἀνέστη γὰρ καὶ 5
ἀπῆλθεν ἐκεῖ ὅθεν ἀπεστάλη. τότε αἱ γυναῖκες φοβηθεῖσαι ἔφυγον.

14 Ἦν δὲ τελευταία ἡμέρα τῶν ἀζύμων, καὶ πολλοί
Lc xxiii 48 τινες ἐξήρχοντο ὑποστρέφοντες εἰς τοὺς οἴκους αὐτῶν, τῆς
ἑορτῆς παυσαμένης. ἡμεῖς δὲ οἱ δώδεκα μαθηταὶ τοῦ 10
Κυρίου ἐκλαίομεν καὶ ἐλυπούμεθα· καὶ ἕκαστος λυπού-
Lc xxiv 14 μενος διὰ τὸ συμβὰν ἀπηλλάγη εἰς τὸν οἶκον αὐτοῦ. ἐγὼ
Jn xxi 2 f. δὲ Σίμων Πέτρος καὶ Ἀνδρέας ὁ ἀδελφός μου λαβόντες
ἡμῶν τὰ λίνα ἀπήλθαμεν εἰς τὴν θάλασσαν· καὶ ἦν σὺν
Mc ii 14 ἡμῖν Λευεὶς ὁ τοῦ Ἀλφαίου, ὃν [ὁ] Κύριος.... 15

4 πιστεύεται ἴδατε 5 ἔστιν] forsitan addendum ὧδε
6 φοβηθεῖς 15 om. ὁ

ΑΠΟΚΑΛΎΨΙΣ ΠΕΤΡΟΥ.

1 ...πολλοὶ ἐξ αὐτῶν ἔσονται ψευδοπροφῆται, καὶ   Mt xxiv 24
ὁδοὺς καὶ δόγματα ποικίλα τῆς ἀπωλείας διδάξουσιν· ἐκεῖνοι Mc xiii 22
δὲ υἱοὶ τῆς ἀπωλείας γενήσονται. καὶ τότε ἐλεύσεται ὁ   Jn xvii 12; 2 Th ii 3
θεὸς ἐπὶ τοὺς πιστούς μου τοὺς πεινῶντας καὶ διψῶντας καὶ Mt v 6
5 θλιβομένους, καὶ ἐν τούτῳ τῷ βίῳ τὰς ψυχὰς ἑαυτῶν δοκι- 2 Th i. 6, 7
μάζοντας· καὶ κρινεῖ τοὺς υἱοὺς τῆς ἀνομίας.

2 Καὶ προσθεὶς ὁ Κύριος ἔφη Ἄγωμεν εἰς τὸ ὄρος   Mt xxvi 30, 45; Mc vi 46; Lc ix 28
[καὶ] εὐξώμεθα. ἀπερχόμενοι δὲ μετ' αὐτοῦ ἡμεῖς οἱ δώ-
δεκα μαθηταὶ ἐδεήθημεν ὅπως δείξῃ ἡμῖν ἕνα τῶν ἀδελφῶν
10 ἡμῶν [τῶν] δικαίων τῶν ἐξελθόντων ἀπὸ τοῦ κόσμου, ἵνα
ἴδωμεν ποταποί εἰσι τὴν μορφήν, καὶ θαρσήσαντες παρα-
θαρσύνωμεν καὶ τοὺς ἀκούοντας ἡμῶν ἀνθρώπους.

3 Καὶ εὐχομένων ἡμῶν ἄ[φνω φαίν]ονται δύο ἄνδρες
ἑστῶτες ἔμπροσθεν τοῦ Κυρίου πρὸς ἔ[ω, οἷς] οὐκ ἐδυνή-
15 θημεν ἀντιβλέψαι· ἐξήρχετο γὰρ ἀπὸ τῆς [ὄ]ψεως αὐτῶν Mt xvii 2, xxviii 3
ἀκτὶν ὡς ἡλίου, καὶ φωτινὸν ἦν αὐ[τῶν ὅλον τὸ] ἔνδυμα,
ὁποῖον οὐδέποτε ὀφθαλμὸς ἀνθρώπ[ου εἶδεν, οὐδὲ] στόμα 1 Cor ii 9
δύναται ἐξηγήσασθαι ἢ καρ[δία ἐκφράσα]ι τὴν δόξαν ἢν

---

2 ποικιλοί   διδάξωσιν ...3 ἀπολείας   4 τοὺς (pr.)] τοῦ
πινῶντας διψῶντας   7 ὄρους εὐζώμεθα   8 ἀπερχόμενος
10 om. τῶν (pr.)   13 α .... φ ... ονται   14 πρὸς ε .... οὐκ
15 τῆς .. ψεως   16 αὐ .... ἔνδυμα
17 ανθρώπ .: .... ρ στόμα   18 ἡ καρ .... ι

ἐνεδέδυντο, καὶ τὸ κάλ[λος τῆς προσό]ψεως ‖ αὐτῶν· οὓς
ἰδόντες ἐθαμβώθημεν· τὰ μὲν γὰρ σώματα αὐτῶν ἦν λευκό-
τερα πάσης χιόνος καὶ ἐρυθρότερα παντὸς ῥόδου, συνεκέ-
κρατο δὲ τὸ ἐρυθρὸν αὐτῶν τῷ λευκῷ, καὶ ἁπλῶς οὐ δύναμαι
ἐξηγήσασθαι τὸ κάλλος αὐτῶν· ἥ τε γὰρ κόμη αὐτῶν οὔλη 5
ἦν καὶ ἀνθηρὰ καὶ ἐπιπρέπουσα αὐτῶν τῷ τε προσώπῳ καὶ
τοῖς ὤμοις, ὡσπερεὶ στέφανος ἐκ ναρδοστάχυος πεπλεγ-
μένος καὶ ποικίλων ἀνθῶν, ἢ ὥσπερ ἶρις ἐν ἀέρι, τοιαύτη
ἦν αὐτῶν ἡ εὐπρέπεια.

4 Ἰδόντες οὖν αὐτῶν τὸ κάλλος ἔκθαμβοι γεγόναμεν 10
πρὸς αὐτούς, ἐπειδὴ ἄφνω ἐφάνησαν, καὶ προσελθὼν τῷ
Κυρίῳ εἶπον Τίνες εἰσὶν οὗτοι; λέγει μοι Οὗτοί εἰσιν οἱ
ἀδελφοὶ ὑμῶν οἱ δίκαιοι ὧν ἠθελήσατε τὰς μορφὰς ἰδεῖν.
κἀγὼ ἔφην αὐτῷ Καὶ ποῦ εἰσι πάντες οἱ δίκαιοι, ἢ ποῖός
ἐστιν ὁ αἰὼν ἐν ᾧ εἰσι ταύτην ἔχοντες τὴν δόξαν ; 15

5 Καὶ ὁ Κύριος ἔδειξέ μοι μέγιστον χῶρον ἐκτὸς
τούτου τοῦ κόσμου ὑπέρλαμπρον τῷ φωτὶ, καὶ τὸν ἀέρα
τὸν ἐκεῖ ἀκτῖσιν ἡλίου καταλαμπόμενον, ‖ καὶ τὴν γῆν
αὐτὴν ἀνθοῦσαν ἀμαράντοις ἄνθεσι, καὶ ἀρωμάτων πλήρη
καὶ φυτῶν εὐανθῶν καὶ ἀφθάρτων καὶ καρπὸν εὐλογημένον 20
φερόντων· τοσοῦτον δὲ ἦν τὸ ἄνθος ὡς καὶ ἐφ' ἡμᾶς ἐκεῖθεν φέρεσθαι. οἱ δὲ οἰκήτορες τοῦ τόπου ἐκείνου ἐνδεδυμένοι ἦσαν ἔνδυμα ἀγγέλων φωτινῶν, καὶ ὅμοιον ἦν τὸ
ἔνδυμα αὐτῶν τῇ χώρᾳ αὐτῶν· ἄγγελοι δὲ περιέτρεχον
αὐτοὺς ἐκεῖσε· ἴση δὲ ἦν ἡ δόξα τῶν ἐκεῖ οἰκητόρων, καὶ 25
μιᾷ φωνῇ τὸν Κύριον θεὸν ἀνευφήμουν, εὐφραινόμενοι
ἐν ἐκείνῳ τῷ τόπῳ. λέγει ἡμῖν ὁ Κύριος Οὗτός ἐστιν ὁ
τόπος τῶν ἀρχέρων ὑμῶν τῶν δικαίων ἀνθρώπων.

Mt xxviii 3

Ecclus l 8

Act iii 11

Apoc vii 13

cf. Mc x 30

1 Pet i 3, v 4

cf. Mt xxii
30 ; Mc xii
25

1 ἀνεδέδυντο   καλω........ψεως   2 λευκότερον
4 τῶν λευκῶν   6 κἂν ἀνθερὰ   7 ὥσπερ εἷς
7, 8 .ναρδοστάχυος πεπλευμένος ....8 τοιαύτην   13 ἡμῶν
22 δὲ οἰκ.] διοικήτορες .. ἐνδεδυμένος   26 τοῦ κυρίου θεοῦ
28 ἀρχέρων] fors. ἀρχιερέων, uel ἀδελφῶν ut supra

6 Εἶδον δὲ καὶ ἕτερον τόπον καταντικρὺς ἐκείνου αὐχμηρὸν πάνυ, καὶ ἦν τόπος κολάσεως· καὶ οἱ κολαζόμενοι
ἐκεῖ καὶ οἱ κολάζοντες ἄγγελοι σκοτινὸν εἶχον αὐτῶν τὸ
ἔνδυμα κατὰ τὸν ἀέρα τοῦ τόπου.

7 Καί τινες ἦσαν ἐκεῖ ἐκ τῆς γλώσσης κρεμάμενοι·
οὗτοι δὲ ἦσαν οἱ βλασφημοῦντες τὴν ὁδὸν τῆς δικαιοσύνης· Mt xxi 32
καὶ ὑπέκειτο αὐτοῖς πῦρ φλεγόμενον καὶ κολάζον αὐτούς.

8 Καὶ λίμνη τις ἦν μεγάλη πεπληρωμένη ‖ βορβόρου Apoc xix 20
φλεγομένου, ἐν ᾧ ἦσαν ἄνθρωποί τινες ἀποστρέφοντες τὴν
δικαιοσύνην, καὶ ἐπέκειντο αὐτοῖς ἄγγελοι βασανισταί.

9 Ἦσαν δὲ καὶ ἄλλαι γυναῖκες τῶν πλοκάμων ἐξηρ- cf. 1 Pet iii 3
τημέναι ἀνωτέρω τοῦ βορβόρου ἐκείνου τοῦ ἀναπαφλά-
ζοντος· αὗτ[αι] δὲ ἦσαν αἱ πρὸς μοιχείαν κοσμηθεῖσαι· οἱ
δὲ συμμι[χθέντες] αὐτῶν τῷ μιάσματι τῆς μοιχείας ἐκ τῶν
ποδῶν [ἦσαν] κ[ρεμάμενοι, καὶ] τὰς κεφαλὰς εἶχον ἐν τῷ
βορβόρ[ῳ, καὶ πάντες] ἔλεγον Οὐκ ἐπιστεύομεν ἐλεύσεσθαι
εἰς τοῦτον τὸν τόπον.

10 Καὶ τοὺς φονεῖς ἔβλεπον καὶ τοὺς συνειδότας
αὐτοῖς βεβλημένους ἔν τινι τόπῳ τεθλιμμένῳ καὶ πεπλη- cf. Mt vii 14
ρωμένῳ ἑρπετῶν πονηρῶν, καὶ πλησσομένους ὑπὸ τῶν Sap Sal xvi 5
θηρίων ἐκείνων, καὶ οὕτω στρεφομένους ἐκεῖ ἐν τῇ κολάσει
ἐκείνῃ· ἐπέκειντο δὲ αὐτοῖς σκώληκες ὥσπερ νεφέλαι Mc ix 44
σκότους. αἱ δὲ ψυχαὶ τῶν πεφονευμένων ἑστῶσαι καὶ
ἐφορῶσαι τὴν κόλασιν ἐκείνων τῶν φονέων ἔλεγον Ὁ θεός, cf. Apoc xvi
δικαία σου ἡ κρίσις. 7 (Ps. xviii
9)

11 Πλησίον δὲ τοῦ τόπου ἐκείνου εἶδον ἕτερον τόπον ‖
τεθλιμμένον, ἐν [ᾧ] ὁ ἰχὼρ καὶ ἡ δυσωδία τῶν κολαζομένων

---

1 ἑταῖρον τόπων   1, 2 αὐχμηρὸν πάνυ] αὐχμηρόντων
3 σκολάζοντες   3, 4 τὸ ἔνδυμα] ἐνδεδυμένα   11 ἄλλοι
13 αἱ] ἦν   14· συμμί[ξαντες]   μοιχείας] μειχίας
15 ποδῶν ∷∷κ.........τὰς   16 βορβόρ[ῳ ....] ἔλεγον
οὐκ ἐπίστευον ἐνελ.   18, 19 συνεισότας αὐτούς   21 οὕτως
τρεφομένους   κολάζει   22 σκόληκες   27 om. ᾧ

κατέρρεε καὶ ὥσπερ λίμνη ἐγίνετο ἐκεῖ· κἀκεῖ ἐκάθηντο
γυναῖκες ἔχουσαι τὸν ἰχῶρα μέχρι τῶν τραχήλων, καὶ
ἀντικρὺς αὐτῶν πολλοὶ παῖδες ο[ἵτινε]ς ἄωροι ἐτίκτοντο
καθήμενοι ἔκλαιον· καὶ προήρχοντο ἐξ αὐ[τῶν φλόγ]ες
πυρὸς καὶ τὰς γυναῖκας ἔπλησσον κατὰ τῶν ὀφθαλμῶν· 5

Sap Sal xii 5 αὗται δὲ ἦσαν α[ἱ τὰ βρέφη φθείρο]υσαι καὶ ἐκτρώ-
σασαι.

12 Καὶ ἕτεροι [ἄνδρες] καὶ γυναῖκες φλεγόμενοι
ἦσαν μέχρι τοῦ ἡμίσους αὐτῶν, καὶ βεβλημένοι ἐν τόπῳ
σκοτινῷ καὶ μαστιζόμενοι ὑπὸ πνευμάτων πονηρῶν, καὶ 10
ἐσθιόμενοι τὰ σπλάγχνα ὑπὸ σκωλήκων ἀκοιμήτων· οὗτοι
δὲ ἦσαν οἱ διώξαντες τοὺς δικαίους καὶ παραδόντες αὐτούς.

13 Καὶ πλησίον ἐκείνων πάλιν γυναῖκες καὶ ἄνδρες
μασώμενοι αὐτῶν τὰ χείλη καὶ κολαζόμενοι, καὶ πεπυρω-
μένον σίδηρον κατὰ τῶν ὀφθαλμῶν λαμβάνοντες· οὗτοι δὲ 15

Act xix 9 ἦσαν οἱ βλασφημήσαντες καὶ κακῶς εἰπόντες τὴν ὁδὸν
τῆς ‖ δικαιοσύνης.

14 Καὶ καταντικρὺ τούτων ἄλλοι πάλιν ἄνδρες καὶ

Apoc xvi 10 γυναῖκες τὰς γλώσσας αὐτῶν μασώμενοι, καὶ πῦρ φλεγόμενον ἔχοντες ἐν τῷ στόματι· οὗτοι δὲ ἦσαν οἱ ψευδομάρ- 20
τυρες.

15 Καὶ ἐν ἑτέρῳ τινὶ τόπῳ χάλικες ἦσαν ὀξύτεροι
ξιφῶν καὶ παντὸς ὀβελίσκου πεπυρωμένοι, καὶ γυναῖκες

Jac ii 2 καὶ ἄνδρες ῥάκη ῥυπαρὰ ἐνδεδυμένοι ἐκυλίοντο ἐπ᾽ αὐτῶν
κολαζόμενοι· οὗτοι δὲ ἦσαν οἱ πλουτοῦντες καὶ τῷ πλούτῳ 25
αὐτῶν πεποιθότες καὶ μὴ ἐλεήσαντες ὀρφανοὺς καὶ χήρας,
ἀλλ᾽ ἀμελήσαντες τῆς ἐντολῆς τοῦ θεοῦ.

16 Ἐν δὲ ἑτέρᾳ λίμνῃ μεγάλῃ πεπληρωμένῃ πίσσης
καὶ αἵματος καὶ βορβόρου ἀναζέοντος ἱστήκεισαν ἄνδρες

3 παῖδες ο..... σα . ωροι   4 αὐ .... ες πυρὸς
6 ἦσαν αρα .... υσαι   8 ἕτεροι ...... καὶ
12 παραδίντες   28 πίσσης] ποίου· fors. πίσσης καὶ θείου.
29 βορβόρῳ ἀναζέοντες

καὶ γυναῖκες μέχρι γονάτων· οὗτοι δὲ ἦσαν οἱ δανίζοντες
καὶ ἀπαιτοῦντες τόκους τόκων.

17 [Καὶ] ἄλλοι ἄνδρες καὶ γυναῖκες ἀπὸ κρημνοῦ
μεγάλου καταστρεφόμενοι ἤρχοντο κάτω, καὶ πάλιν
5 ἐλαύνοντο ὑπὸ τῶν ἐπικειμένων ἀναβῆναι ἄνω ‖ ἐπὶ τοῦ
κρημνοῦ, καὶ κατεστρέφοντο, ἐκεῖθεν κάτω, καὶ ἡσυχίαν
οὐκ εἶχον ἀπὸ ταύτης τῆς κολάσεως· οὗτοι δὲ ἦσαν οἱ
μιάναντες τὰ σώματα ἑαυτῶν ὡς γυναῖκες ἀναστρεφόμενοι·
αἱ δὲ μετ᾽ αὐτῶν γυναῖκες, αὗται ἦσαν αἱ συγκοιμηθεῖσαι
10 ἀλλήλαις ὡς ἂν ἀνὴρ πρὸς γυναῖκα.

18 Καὶ παρὰ τῷ κρημνῷ ἐκείνῳ τόπος ἦν πυρὸς
πλείστου γέμων, κἀκεῖ ἱστήκεισαν ἄνδρες οἵτινες ταῖς ἰδίαις
χερσὶ ξόανα ἑαυτοῖς ἐποίησαν ἀντὶ θεοῦ.

19 Καὶ παρ᾽ ἐκείνοις ἄνδρες ἕτεροι καὶ γυναῖκες
15 ῥάβδους ἔχοντες καὶ ἀλλήλους τύπτοντες καὶ μηδέποτε
παυόμενοι τῆς τοιαύτης κολάσεως.

20 Καὶ ἕτεροι πάλιν ἐγγὺς ἐκείνων γυναῖκες καὶ
ἄνδρες φλεγόμενοι καὶ στρεφόμενοι καὶ τηγανιζόμενοι·
οὗτοι δὲ ἦσαν οἱ ἀφέντες τὴν ὁδὸν τοῦ θεοῦ....

cf. Apoc. xiv
11
Rom i 26, 27

Mc vii 8

3 [καὶ] ἄλλοι] ἀλλὰ   6 καταστρέφοντο   11, 12 πυρὸς
πλείστου γέμων] πρὸς πλείστου γενῶν   19 ἀφέντες] ἄφθαντες

FRAGMENTS OF THE REVELATION.

1. [This and the following fragment probably preceded our text.]

a. Περιουσίας δ᾽ ἕνεκεν λελέχθω κἀκεῖνο τὸ λελεγμένον ἐν τῇ Ἀποκαλύψει τοῦ Πέτρου. εἰσάγει τὸν οὐρανὸν ἅμα τῇ γῇ κριθήσεσθαι οὕτως· Ἡ γῆ, φησί, παραστήσει πάντας τῷ θεῷ ἐν ἡμέρᾳ κρίσεως καὶ αὐτὴ μέλλουσα κρίνεσθαι σὺν καὶ τῷ περιέχοντι οὐρανῷ. Macarius Magnes *Apocritica* iv. 6, p. 164.

b. Ἡ γῆ—θεῷ κρινομένους—κρίσεως, μέλλουσα καὶ αὐτὴ— οὐρανῷ. ut supra, *op. cit.* iv. 16, p. 185.

2. Καὶ ἐκεῖνο δ᾽ αὖθις λέγει, ὃ καὶ ἀσεβείας μεστὸν ὑπάρχει τὸ ῥῆμα φάσκον· Καὶ τακήσεται πᾶσα δύναμις οὐρανοῦ, καὶ ἑλιχθήσεται ὁ οὐρανὸς ὡς βιβλίον, καὶ πάντα τὰ ἄστρα πεσεῖται ὡς φύλλα ἐξ ἀμπέλου, καὶ ὡς πίπτει φύλλα ἀπὸ συκῆς. *op. cit.* iv. 7, p. 165.

Compare Isa. xxxiv. 4.

3. [Probably this and the following fragments are to be placed either in or after our text.]

Ἡ γραφή φησι τὰ βρέφη τὰ ἐκτεθέντα τημελούχῳ παραδίδοσθαι ἀγγέλῳ, ὑφ᾽ οὗ παιδεύεσθαί τε καὶ αὔξειν· καὶ ἔσονται, φησίν, ὡς οἱ ἑκατὸν ἐτῶν ἐνταῦθα πιστοί. Clem. Alex. *Eclogae ex Scriptt. Proph.* xli.

4. Διὸ καὶ Πέτρος ἐν τῇ Ἀποκαλύψει φησί· Καὶ ἀστραπὴ πυρὸς πηδῶσα ἀπὸ τῶν βρεφῶν ἐκείνων καὶ

πλήσσουσα τοὺς ὀφθαλμοὺς τῶν γυναικῶν. Clem. Alex. l.c. Cf. § 11 of our text. This 41st section of Clement's *Eclogae* has been hitherto looked upon as one and continuous: it appears to me clear that it consists of two parts.

5 *a*. (cf. 3) Αὐτίκα ὁ Πέτρος ἐν τῇ Ἀποκαλύψει φησὶν τὰ βρέφη [τὰ] ἐξαμβλωθέντα τῆς ἀμείνονος ἐσόμενα μοίρας [*cod.* πείρας]· ταῦτα ἀγγέλῳ τημελούχῳ παραδίδοσθαι, ἵνα γνώσεως μεταλαβόντα τῆς ἀμείνονος τύχῃ μονῆς, παθόντα ἃ ἂν ἔπαθεν καὶ ἐν σώματι γενόμενα· τὰ δ᾽ ἕτερα μόνης τῆς σωτηρίας τεύξεται, ὡς ἠδικημένα ἐλεηθέντα, καὶ μένει (*or* μενεῖ) ἄνευ κολάσεως, τοῦτο γέρας λαβόντα. Clem. Alex. l.c. xlviii.

5 *b*. Ὅθεν δὴ καὶ τημελούχοις ἀγγέλοις, κἂν ἐκ μοιχείας ὦσι, τὰ ἀποτικτόμενα παραδίδοσθαι παρειλήφαμεν ἐν θεοπνεύστοις γράμμασιν. εἰ γὰρ παρὰ τὴν γνώμην ἐγίνοντο καὶ τὸν θεσμὸν τῆς μακαρίας ἐκείνης φύσεως τοῦ θεοῦ, πῶς ἀγγέλοις ταῦτα παρεδίδοτο τραφησόμενα μετὰ πολλῆς ἀναπαύσεως καὶ ῥᾳστώνης; πῶς δὲ καὶ κατηγορήσοντα σφῶν αὐτῶν τοὺς γονεῖς εὐπαρρησιάστως εἰς τὸ δικαστήριον ἐκίκλησκον τοῦ Χριστοῦ· Σὺ οὐκ ἐφθόνησας ἡμῖν, ὦ Κύριε, τὸ κοινόν, λέγοντα, τοῦτο φῶς· οὗτοι δὲ ἡμᾶς εἰς θάνατον ἐξέθεντο, καταφρονήσαντες τῆς σῆς ἐντολῆς. S. Methodius, *Conviv. Virg.* ii. 6.

6. Τὸ δὲ γάλα τῶν γυναικῶν ῥέον ἀπὸ τῶν μαστῶν καὶ πηγνύμενον, φησὶν ὁ Πέτρος ἐν τῇ Ἀποκαλύψει, γεννήσει θηρία λεπτὰ σαρκοφάγα, καὶ ἀνατρέχοντα εἰς αὐτὰς κατεσθίει· διὰ τὰς ἁμαρτίας γίνεσθαι τὰς κολάσεις διδάσκων. ἐκ τῶν ἁμαρτιῶν γεννᾶσθαι αὐτάς φησιν, ὡς διὰ τὰς ἁμαρτίας ἐπράθη ὁ λαός, καὶ διὰ τὴν εἰς Χριστὸν ἀπιστίαν, ὡς φησὶν ὁ Ἀπόστολος, ὑπὸ τῶν ὄφεων ἐδάκνοντο (1 Cor. x. 9). Clem. Alex. *op. cit.* xlix.

Sap Sal xvi 1, 2
2 Pet ii 19 6

7. The following passage may probably contain an allusion to the Apocalypse:

Εἴπομεν ὡς κολάσεις εἰσὶ βλασφημιῶν, φλυαρίας, ἀκολάστων ῥημάτων, λόγῳ κολαζομένων καὶ παιδευομένων. ἔφασκεν δὲ [*sc.* ὁ πρεσβύτης : cf. § l.] καὶ διὰ τὰς τρίχας κολάζεσθαι καὶ τὸν κόσμον τὰς γυναῖκας ὑπὸ δυνάμεως τῆς ἐπὶ τούτοις τεταγμένης, ἢ καὶ τῷ Σαμψὼν δύναμιν παρεῖχε ταῖς θριξίν, ἥτις κολάζει τὰς διὰ κόσμου τριχῶν ἐπὶ πορνείαν ὁρμώσας.

Clem. Alex. *op. cit.* xxxix., xl. The latter half of § xxxix. should evidently be joined to § xl.

CAMBRIDGE: PRINTED BY C. J. CLAY & SONS, AT THE UNIVERSITY PRESS.

TEXTS AND STUDIES.

ıtributions to Biblical and Patristic Literature. Edited by J. ARMITAGE ROBINSON, B.D., Fellow of Christ's College.

The following numbers of the series are now published:

. I. No. 1. THE APOLOGY OF ARISTIDES: by J. RENDEL HARRIS, M.A.: with an Appendix by THE EDITOR. Second Edition. 5s. *net.*

No. 2. THE PASSION OF S. PERPETUA, with an Appendix on the Scillitan Martyrdom: by THE EDITOR. 4s. *net.*

No. 3. THE LORD'S PRAYER IN THE EARLY CHURCH: by F. H. CHASE, B.D. 5s. *net.*

No. 4. THE FRAGMENTS OF HERACLEON: by A. E. BROOKE, M.A. 4s. *net.*

. II. No. 1. A STUDY OF CODEX BEZAE: by J. RENDEL HARRIS, M.A. 7s. 6d. *net.*

No. 2. THE TESTAMENT OF ABRAHAM: by M. R. JAMES, M.A., with an Appendix by W. E. BARNES, B.D. 5s. *net.*

A separate title page for binding is issued with the last number each volume.

The following are in course of preparation:

THE RULES OF TYCONIUS: freshly edited from the MSS, with an examination of his witness to the Old Latin Version: by F. C. BURKITT, M.A. [*In the Press.*

APOCRYPHA ANECDOTA: containing the Latin Version of the Apocalypse of Paul, the Apocalypses of the Virgin, of Sedrach, of Zosimas, &c.: by M. R. JAMES, M.A. [*In the Press.*

London: C. J. CLAY AND SONS,
CAMBRIDGE UNIVERSITY PRESS WAREHOUSE,
AVE MARIA LANE.

Bringing Classics to Life

BOOK JUNGLE

www.bookjungle.com *email: sales@bookjungle.com fax: 630-214-0564 mail: Book Jungle PO Box 2226 Champaign, IL 61825*

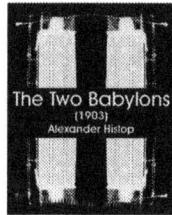

The Two Babylons
Alexander Hislop

QTY

You may be surprised to learn that many traditions of Roman Catholicism in fact don't come from Christ's teachings but from an ancient Babylonian "Mystery" religion that was centered on Nimrod, his wife Semiramis, and a child Tammuz. This book shows how this ancient religion transformed itself as it incorporated Christ into its teachings....

Religion/History   **Pages:358**

ISBN: *1-59462-010-5*   *MSRP $22.95*

The Power Of Concentration
Theron Q. Dumont

It is of the utmost value to learn how to concentrate. To make the greatest success of anything you must be able to concentrate your entire thought upon the idea you are working on. The person that is able to concentrate utilizes all constructive thoughts and shuts out all destructive ones...

Self Help/Inspirational   **Pages:196**

ISBN: *1-59462-141-1*   *MSRP $14.95*

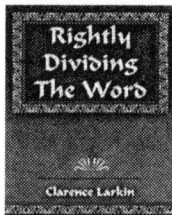

Rightly Dividing The Word
Clarence Larkin

The "Fundamental Doctrines" of the Christian Faith are clearly outlined in numerous books on Theology, but they are not available to the average reader and were mainly written for students. The Author has made it the work of his ministry to preach the "Fundamental Doctrines." To this end he has aimed to express them in the simplest and clearest manner..

Religion   **Pages:352**

ISBN: *1-59462-334-1*   *MSRP $23.45*

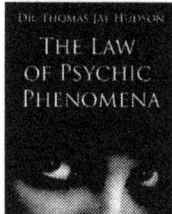

The Law of Psychic Phenomena
Thomson Jay Hudson

"I do not expect this book to stand upon its literary merits; for if it is unsound in principle, felicity of diction cannot save it, and if sound, homeliness of expression cannot destroy it. My primary object in offering it to the public is to assist in bringing Psychology within the domain of the exact sciences. That this has never been accomplished..."

New Age   **Pages:420**

ISBN: *1-59462-124-1*   *MSRP $29.95*

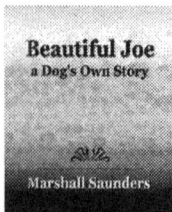

Beautiful Joe
Marshall Saunders

When Marshall visited the Moore family in 1892, she discovered Joe, a dog they had nursed back to health from his previous abusive home to live a happy life. So moved was she, that she wrote this classic masterpiece which won accolades and was recognized as a heartwarming symbol for humane animal treatment...

Fiction   **Pages:256**

ISBN: *1-59462-261-2*   *MSRP $18.45*

Bringing Classics to Life   BOOK JUNGLE
www.bookjungle.com *email: sales@bookjungle.com fax: 630-214-0564 mail: Book Jungle PO Box 2226*
Champaign, IL 61825

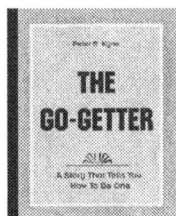

The Go-Getter
Kyne B. Peter

QTY

The Go Getter is the story of William Peck.He was a war
veteran and amputee who will not be refused what he wants.
Peck not only fights to find employment but continually
proves himself more than competent at the many difficult test
that are throw his way in the course of his early days with the
Ricks Lumber Company...

Business/Self Help/Inspirational   Pages:68
ISBN: *1-59462-186-1*   *MSRP* **$8.95**

Self Mastery
Emile Coue

Emile Coue came up with novel way to improve the lives of
people. He was a pharmacist by trade and often saw ailing
people. This lead him to develop autosuggestion, a form of
self-hypnosis. At the time his theories weren't popular but
over the years evidence is mounting that he was indeed right
all along...

New Age/Self Help   Pages:98
ISBN: *1-59462-189-6*   *MSRP* **$7.95**

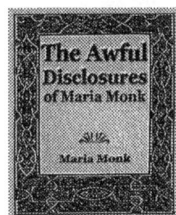

The Awful Disclosures Of
Maria Monk

"I cannot banish the scenes and characters of this book
from my memory. To me it can never appear like an amus-
ing fable, or lose its interest and importance. The story
is one which is continually before me, and must return
fresh to my mind with painful emotions as long as I live..."

Religion   Pages:232
ISBN: *1-59462-160-8*   *MSRP* **$17.95**

As a Man Thinketh
James Allen

"This little volume (the result of meditation and experience)
is not intended as an exhaustive treatise on the much-writ-
ten-upon subject of the power of thought. It is suggestive
rather than explanatory, its object being to stimulate men
and women to the discovery and perception of the truth that
by virtue of the thoughts which they choose and encourage..."

Inspirational/Self Help   Pages:80
ISBN: *1-59462-231-0*   *MSRP* **$9.45**

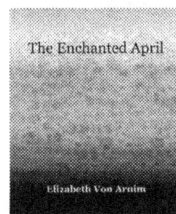

The Enchanted April
Elizabeth Von Arnim

It began in a woman's club in London on a February
afternoon, an uncomfortable club, and a miserable afternoon when Mrs. Wilkins, who had come down from
Hampstead to shop and had lunched at her club, took
up The Times from the table in the smoking-room...

Fiction   Pages:368
ISBN: *1-59462-150-0*   *MSRP* **$23.45**

Bringing Classics to Life

BOOK JUNGLE

www.bookjungle.com *email: sales@bookjungle.com fax: 630-214-0564 mail: Book Jungle PO Box 2226 Champaign, IL 61825*

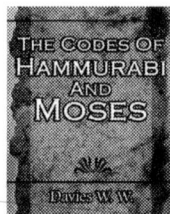

The Codes Of Hammurabi And Moses - W. W. Davies

The discovery of the Hammurabi Code is one of the greatest achievements of archaeology, and is of paramount interest, not only to the student of the Bible, but also to all those interested in ancient history...

Religion   **Pages:132**

ISBN: *1-59462-338-4*   *MSRP* **$12.95**

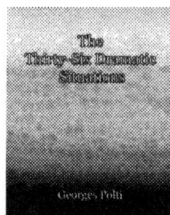

The Thirty-Six Dramatic Situations
Georges Polti

An incredibly useful guide for aspiring authors and playwrights. This volume categorizes every dramatic situation which could occur in a story and describes them in a list of 36 situations. A great aid to help inspire or formalize the creative writing process...

Self Help/Reference   **Pages:204**

ISBN: *1-59462-134-9*   *MSRP* **$15.95**

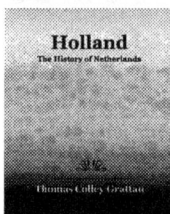

Holland - The History Of Netherlands
Thomas Colley Grattan

Thomas Grattan was a prestigious writer from Dublin who served as British Consul to the US. Among his works is an authoritative look at the history of Holland. A colorful and interesting look at history....

History/Politics   **Pages:408**

ISBN: *1-59462-137-3*   *MSRP* **$26.95**

A Concise Dictionary of Middle English
A. L. Mayhew
Walter W. Skeat

The present work is intended to meet, in some measure, the requirements of those who wish to make some study of Middle-English, and who find a difficulty in obtaining such assistance as will enable them to find out the meanings and etymologies of the words most essential to their purpose...

Reference/History   **Pages:332**

ISBN: *1-59462-119-5*   *MSRP* **$29.95**

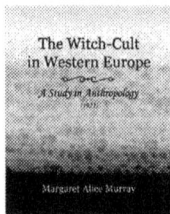

The Witch-Cult in Western Europe
Margaret Murray

QTY

The mass of existing material on this subject is so great that I have not attempted to make a survey of the whole of European "Witchcraft" but have confined myself to an intensive study of the cult in Great Britain. In order, however, to obtain a clearer understanding of the ritual and beliefs I have had recourse to French and Flemish sources...

Occult   **Pages:308**

ISBN: *1-59462-126-8*   *MSRP* **$22.45**

Bringing Classics to Life

BOOK JUNGLE

www.bookjungle.com *email: sales@bookjungle.com fax: 630-214-0564 mail: Book Jungle PO Box 2226 Champaign, IL 61825*

Name	
Email	
Telephone	
Address	
City, State ZIP	

☐ **Credit Card**   ☐ **Check / Money Order**

Credit Card Number	
Expiration Date	
Signature	

Please Mail to: Book Jungle
PO Box 2226
Champaign, IL 61825
or Fax to: 630-214-0564

ORDERING INFORMATION

web*: www.bookjungle.com*
email*: sales@bookjungle.com*
fax*: 630-214-0564*
mail*: Book Jungle PO Box 2226 Champaign, IL 61825*
or PayPal *to sales@bookjungle.com*

Please contact us for bulk discounts
DIRECT-ORDER TERMS

20% Discount if You Order
Two or More Books
Free Domestic Shipping!